Vending Machine Business Secrets (2022)

How to Start & Scale Your Vending Business From $0 to Passive Income – Comprehensive Guide with Case Studies, Best Machines to Buy, Location Negotiation & More!

Written by Carter Woods

**For your free downloadable vending machine contract template, go to
CarterWoodsVending.Carrd.co**

Disclaimer & Copyright

© COPYRIGHT 2022 Carter Woods– All rights reserved

The content contained within this book may not be reproduced, duplicated or transmitted without direct written permission from the author or the publisher.

Under no circumstances will any blame or legal responsibility be held against the publisher, or author, for any damages, reparation, or monetary loss due to the information contained within this book. Either directly or indirectly. You are responsible for your own choices, actions, and results.

Legal Notice:

This book is copyright protected. This book is only for personal use. You cannot amend, distribute, sell, use, quote or paraphrase any part, or the content within this book, without the consent of the author or publisher.

Disclaimer Notice:

Please note the information contained within this document is for educational and entertainment purposes only. All effort has been executed to present accurate, up to date, and reliable, complete information. No warranties of any kind are declared or implied. Readers acknowledge that the author is not engaging in the rendering of legal, financial, medical or professional advice. The content within this book has been derived from various sources. Please consult a licensed professional before attempting any techniques outlined in this book.

By reading this document, the reader agrees that under no circumstances is the author responsible for any losses, direct or indirect, which are incurred as a result of the use of the information contained within this document, including, but not limited to, — errors, omissions, or inaccuracies.

Table of Contents

Introduction 4

Chapter 1: Why Start a Vending Machine Business? 9

Chapter 2: Researching Your Area and First Tasks 19

Chapter 3: Opening Your LLC & Getting Your Equipment 45

Chapter 4: Negotiating With Local Businesses and Tactics For Securing Locations/Routes 75

Chapter 5: Operational Management, Security, and Profit Margins 81

Chapter 6: General Business and Tax Advice 99

Chapter 7: Insider Secrets From My Experience & Deal Analysis 131

Chapter 8: The Future Of The Vending Machine Industry 155

Chapter 9: Re-Investing & Scaling Your Business to Six-Figures a Year 164

Chapter 10: A Potential New Business Model For 2022/2023 180

Conclusion 202

Introduction

"You can only have one job, but you can have unlimited vending machines."

Carter Woods, Author

Like most individuals, you are probably stuck in your 9-5 job, and you are looking for an escape. You might have heard of the vending machine industry and that it is a potentially profitable side hustle. You may have tried other business ventures in the past but have failed for any number of reasons, and you have decided that this could be the venture for you, and you are determined to make this work. You may not know where to buy your first vending machines or what capital you might need to get started and get your business off the ground. You may also not know how to run the business, and you would like to learn from someone who has done it before and has been through all the trials and tribulations.

The solutions to your problems are all contained within this book, from lack of money, wanting to start a business, quitting your job, where to start, or how much it is going to cost. This book has everything you need to get started on your venture and make it a success with all the insider secrets you could ever need. After you have read this book, you will be able to start your vending machine side-hustle and eventually, within a few months, turn it into a full-time business. A profitable vending machine business will provide you with a stable cash flow to provide for your family and put food on the table. It will also allow you to live the lifestyle you desire, free from financial stress, an unfulfilling job, and a condescending boss. Like many individuals, you may be drawn to the simplicity, predictability, and reliability of the cash flow this business provides, and you are eager to learn more about the ins and outs. With the flexibility of starting this business within your hometown, regardless of how big or small it may be. With a vending machine business, you can create long-lasting relationships with business owners to successfully place your machines on their premises.

I, Carter Woods, have had experience in the vending industry for the past few years, and I will teach you everything you need to know, from what to stock in your machines, which contracts to use, how to approach locations owners, how to price your products, file taxes, reinvest and scale your business to make six figures in profit. I decided to write this book because I have been asked about my vending machine business by a variety of people in the past. Individuals are curious about the industry and want to get into it, so I have decided to share my expertise. I have a ton of knowledge and made a significant amount of money along the way. I intend to show you what not to do so you don't make the same mistakes as I did while still making money.

You will receive the following benefits from reading this book

- The concept behind vending machines

- How the business model works
- Know the types of vending machines available
- The benefits of vending machines
- An overview of the industry
- How to get started
- What to name your business
- What to consider
- Purchasing a vending route
- Avoiding scam
- Finding the perfect location
- Contracts and customer service
- Marketing guide for vending business
- Essentials
- Questions to ask yourself
- Legal stuff
- Financing and leasing machines
- Value of a location
- Vending for profit
- Myths about the vending business

Consider the following questions before you start your vending machine business:

Are you creating a business plan? Even though this might not seem important, it is in fact one of the most important aspects of a successful business along with a business profile. Many individuals think it's the same thing, but they are pretty different. A business plan will ultimately make or break your business because it will set aside the key factors of your business and how you would like your business to be run.

What would you want to gain from vending? What are your main goals with your vending machine business? It could be that you like the idea of working for yourself or to have your very own small business. Determine why you are interested in starting your own vending machine business. This will ultimately form the way that you start your business, should you want to start the business to make extra income, then your business structure will be very different from the person who would like to do the business as an aid to early retirement. Keep the following challenges in mind and be sure that you are up to it before starting your business:

- Are you willing to work long hours?
- Are you able to talk with and manage other people?
- Would you mind doing physical activities from time to time?
- Are you willing to drive a lot?
- Will you be able to stay patient while your business is growing?

Whether you see the previous questions as pros or cons is entirely up to you, but they are still essential to consider. Lay out everything you want from your business on paper and take it from there.

Will you actually receive an income? Keeping proper track of your business through keeping track of the money you are receiving from your machines and the money you are putting out for maintenance and restocking is important to the growth of your business. You also need to ensure that your products are priced just right to ensure that you are actually making a profit from them, and this should be enough to cover all of your expenses related to the business.

Do you have the necessary skills? Some may believe that running a vending machine business only means that you need to restock your machines and collect money, but the truth is there is a lot more involved in running a successful business. You need to have physical strength and stamina, be able to deal with stress, be good with other people, and have the necessary analytical skills with regard to products. Not to mention you need to have the necessary math skills. Now you may feel a bit overwhelmed with all of this, but just know that with the information contained here, you will be able to make a success of your business.

Chapter 1:
Why Start a Vending Machine Business?

"What do you need to start a business? Three simple things: know your product better than anyone, know your customer, and have a burning desire."

Dave Thomas

The vending machine business has shown to be highly lucrative over the past few years, with more individuals seeking to join the industry. I have decided to give you an indication of what this industry involves. The vending machine business can be customized according to your location and your clients. Business owners are filling their vending machines with anything from soda, snacks, DVDs, facemasks, and even cosmetic products and toiletries. Vending machine owners are required to purchase, maintain, and supply their machines to their clients. Starting this business requires that you keep three things in mind at all times: location, products, and sustainability. It's a clever move to only start purchasing your vending tools and materials after you have secured your locations unless you are buying existing routes, which we will get to later on in the book. The vending machine industry is growing substantially and more and more people are looking at getting into the game.

To get into the financial aspect of owning a vending machine business, according to researchers, the vending machine business was valued at $18,28 billion in 2019 and is suspected to reach $25,25 billion by 2027. The Compound Annual Growth Rate (CAGR) is estimated to be around 6.7% from 2021 to 2027. The revenue possibility is estimated to be around $6.97 billion from 2019 to 2027. With the advancement in technology related to vending machines, owners will soon be able to gather valuable information about consumers, including customer experiences and expectations, and this improves their overall shopping experience. The beverage vending machine industry has been dominating and is used in a variety of applications, like hotels and restaurants, corporate offices, and supermarkets, among others, and is expected to keep growing in the near future.

There are a few benefits to investing in a vending machine business that makes them highly profitable for the owner of the business. The most significant benefits are:

• Your attention won't be needed full-time with a vending business. As long as you ensure your machines are serviced regularly, stocked when needed, and you collect the money, the business runs itself and makes you profit while you sleep. You can set up your schedule to suit your current commitments to ensure it doesn't interfere with your existing routine. Once you are set up and making enough profit you can decide to employ someone to manage your machines, which frees up your time even more.

• You don't need to have extensive experience in the business to enter it, although you might want to familiarize yourself with the basic concepts of the business before investing. Knowledge is key, although you can go for training and educate yourself along the way.

- Profit is immediate - With vending machines being cash-only you will not have the struggle of collecting money from individuals.

- The overall cost of running your vending machine business is very low; the only running costs you may have to cover are traveling to and from your machines and restocking them, which are covered by the profit you make.

- When you provide the most purchased items through your vending machine, you will be sure to always make a profit. People often buy their favorites from vending machines and tend not to deviate from their preferences.

- The vending machine industry is very diversified as individuals come up with more unique products to add to their machines to increase sales.

- The predictability of the business is easy. With the need for cashless purchases increasing over the past two years, the vending machine business has grown significantly. Individuals are preferring to purchase products from machines as opposed to in-person purchases.

- The fact stands as with any business; if you run it correctly, the amount of profit you will be able to generate is endless. The current state of the industry is a clear indication of the profitability of this business structure.

- The scalability of the business is a big advantage

for owners. As the demand for your machines and the products you provide grows, you can increase the number of machines you have and, through this, grow your business to significant heights while increasing profits. You will be able to cover more locations when you increase the number of machines you have, and this will create more exposure for clients to get in contact with you.

- Due to the nature of the business, it's easy to start a vending machine business. With no employees or office space needed, you can put all your attention into finding locations or available routes to get your business operating.

Although there are many many business models that you might be looking into when you want to start your own business, you need to keep a few things in mind about the vending machine business. For this, I will use the comparison between the dropshipping and vending machine business models. While dropshipping may be a more accessible business to start, you need to know that the industry is highly saturated, and your chances of making a profit are meager. You need to know that there are hundreds if not thousands of other individuals selling the same products that you are. With the vending machine business depending on your creativity, you can scale this business as you see fit and make your vending machines as unique as possible.

The other thing about the dropshipping business is to start you would need to have a website or other advertising platform ready before you start so you can refer individuals to purchase the products from you. Vending machines may require that you go out and look for new business opportunities or locations, but the market is large with new locations becoming available daily. You would need to grow your communication skills with the vending business model to get new clients, but once they use your machines, you will start making a profit. Another big benefit of the vending machine model is that it has one of the highest profit margins as opposed to any other business model, with a dropshipping business having low or no profit margin.

The vending machine business is preferred by many individuals for various reasons. Unlike other passive income streams, you work according to your schedule, and the business does not require any advertising, although you can advertise on your machines if needed. The income received from this business model is limitless, and it builds your personality and morale as a business owner. A vending machine also works for you 24 hours a day, seven days a week, without you having to motivate it, and does not take sick leave days, coffee breaks, or have unpredictable performance.

As with any business, there are a few drawbacks concerning the vending machine business, but they are not significant and can be easily overcome with the right planning. Getting started with the business could mean that you would need to have funds to cover the start-up. A new machine costs around $3,000 depending on the machine you would like to purchase, as well as paying a percentage to the owner of a location you have placed a machine. These costs can easily be planned for before you start the business and be calculated in your planning.

Another big drawback with this business is the

security aspect of placing your machines. Should your machine be placed in a public place, you need to ensure that your machines are protected, you may install cameras, but to increase security, you can add glass to only give clients access to the payment and dispersal slots. Your travel expenses may also cut into your profit; this includes the restocking of items and maintaining your machines multiple times a week. You may also incur expenses related to repairing your machine that may cut into your profits. This can be prevented if you make a provision every month to cover not only travel expenses but also major repairs that may happen unexpectedly. Stocking your machines will need extensive market research to ensure that the products your machines are filled with will be sold and won't be sitting for days or weeks.

When thinking about who this business is best for, then the simple answer would be absolutely anyone who is willing to work on their business. This business model is not biased based on age or gender and literally anyone can get involved. There are vending machine business owners who are actively involving their children in the daily running of their businesses to teach them all the tools of the trade so they can one day take over the business. As long as you can hustle and you have a desire for success, then you can make this business model work for you.

Let's get into the profitability margins of the business model. A single vending machine, when, for example, placed in a busy hotel with no restaurant, can make a few hundred dollars a day. In contrast, a machine in an apartment basement can only make a few dollars a month. The profit of a vending machine depends on a variety of different factors, including the type of machine, location, products provided, and the price of the items. Diversifying your products and machines can bring in a higher profit margin and increase your earnings.

For example, if you have a well placed vending machine selling only snacks, and this machine sells upwards of 50 items a day at $4 each, but you only paid 50 cents per snack, then your profits will be around $175 should you have several popular, well-placed machines then your earnings will be worth your effort. As with any business, it takes a significant amount of effort to make it a success.

When we look at the profit margins for a soda vending machine, we can calculate the income with the following formula; note the amounts used are purely for example purposes:

- Purchase price: $0.38 per can
- Selling price: $1.00 per can
- Profit: $0.62 per can

Should your machine sell 50 units per day, your profit will be as follows

- Per day: $31.00
- Per week: $217
- Per month: $868
- Per year: $10,416

Should you own ten machines, your monthly profit will be approximately: $8,680 per month.

Candy vending machines

- Purchase price: $0.73
- Selling Price: $1.50
- Profit: $0.77

Should your machine sell 50 units per day, your profit will be as follows:

- Per day: $38.50
- Per week: $269.50
- Per month: $1078.00
- Per year: $12,936

Should you own ten machines, your monthly profit will be approximately: $10,780 per month.

Snack vending machines (Chips)

- Purchase price: $0.32
- Selling price: $0.75
- Profit: $0.43

Should your machine sell 50 units per day, your profit will be as follows:

- Per day: $21.50
- Per week: $150.50
- Per month: $602.00
- Per year: $7,224

Should you own ten machines, your monthly profit will be approximately: $6,020 per month.

Selling a vending route can be time-consuming, overwhelming, and confusing if not handled properly. Following the tips listed below will help make the process much easier and more successful:

Financial records: Keeping up-to-date financial records is important information to sell a vending machine business/route. Newer vending machines can provide a gross sales report, but some older machines require manual financial reporting. Cash purchases can sometimes not provide the proof of sales needed to draft proper financial reports. You need to however keep a detailed list of sales information for at least six months, and this needs to be broken down according to location, cash vs. credit cards, date of collection, etc.

Contact information: Buyers will be more willing to consider purchasing a route if the information for existing contracts is already in place. Having this information available is imperative to make sure the transition proceeds as smoothly as possible.

Third-party sales company: When you find the prospect of selling a route to be daunting, then you may want to consider hiring a third-party company that will help you to find qualified buyers. They can request financial information from buyers to ensure they qualify for the purchase of your route. Some companies advertise your route and only require compensation when a buyer is approved and the route is sold.

Document machines and equipment: Buyers often require proof that the machines are operational and in excellent condition. Taking photos of your machines in their current locations will give them peace of mind that the offer is legitimate.

Realistic expectations: Routes are often sold at 1 - 2 times the annual gross sales. For example, if a route brings in $10,00 in sales, then the expected selling price of the route will be around $5,000 to $10,000. This is variable, but it should be the expectation. The value of the equipment is often not considered, but buyers will more than likely pay $1,000 for a used machine than purchase an overpriced route because of equipment.

There are other variables to consider when selling your route, but this is a good start when you are considering selling your route.

There is absolutely no doubt that this is a great business model and opportunity for you to start your own business, whether you start it right now or once you finish listening to the podcast or reading this book. The best time to start is right now.

Here is a question I received from a potential vending machine business owner. He has been researching business ideas that don't require too much capital to begin with and can be somewhat automated/part-time; as he was looking, he found vending to be surprisingly the best fit and potentially very profitable as well. His intentions are to grow the business into more than just a side-income gig. But now he has the following questions about where he should start?

- Brand new machines: There are around $4,000 - $6,000 each, and then you need to find locations and inventory management software. There are people offering location services for between $500 and $1,000 per location. The uncertainty is holding him off.

- Brand new machines with business support: When using this option, machines are around $10,000 to $11,000. Companies offering this often require that you pay before the company starts finding locations, not to mention that these companies require that you purchase between 3 and 5 machines. The machines often have a 4 - 8 week lead time. The payment terms on this option are holding him back.

- Used machines: Same uncertainties as with the first option, although the capital required is much lower, normally between $1,000 to $3,000 per machine.

Now his question to me was which option would I recommend and do I have any experience with locating services. Also, was getting an inventory app worth it when he has less than five machines?

Well, my recommendation was to stay away from the second option. Purchasing used machines is typically the best option when starting out, although should you not have the necessary technical/mechanical skills, then you might want to get into contact with a good refurbisher in your area. New machines are a great option when you have the capital to invest, but you need to keep in mind that your return on investment needs to cover your new machine costs, and you might have to wait a bit longer before you see an actual income.

Chapter 2:

Researching Your Area and First Tasks

"Make the most of yourself by fanning the tiny, inner sparks of possibility into flames of achievement."

Golda Meir

Registering your vending machine business as an LLC (or LTD should you be located in the United Kingdom) is likely the best option, especially because you will be working with food-related products. An LLC protects your personal assets like your car, house, and savings in the event of being sued or when your business defaults on debts. The cost of registering an LLC depends on the state you are residing in and ranges between $40 and $500. Registering as an LLC is the most cost-effective option, especially when you are looking for the protection of your personal assets. The main benefits of registering your vending machine business as an LLC are: protection for your personal assets with limited liability protection, more tax benefits and options, and increased business credibility. Another significant benefit of an LLC is that it will be taxed as a pass-through entity, which means the business income will pass through the owner's individual tax return. The business income is subject to income taxes and self-employment taxes. With the credibility an LLC provides, a vending machine business owner can gain customers' trust more quickly. Forming an LLC can be done in a few easy steps:

- **Step 1:** Select your state. You should choose the state where you are currently living and planning to establish your company.

- **Step 2:** Choosing your name. You would need to choose a unique and distinguishable name for your business that will set you aside from the existing businesses in your area. Once you have decided on your company name, you can proceed to design your logo, which you will be using to advertise your business.

- **Step 3:** Choose an agent. When you partner with an LLC registered agent, they will work with any legal documentation and tax notices for you.

- **Step 4:** File your articles of organization. Also known as a Certificate of Formation is a document you need to file to officially register your business with the state.

- **Step 5:** LLC Operating Agreement. This is a legal document that needs to be drawn up to identify and outline the owners and duties of your LLC.

- **Step 6:** EIN. Employer Identification Number is used by the US Internal Revenue Service to identify and tax businesses. Simply put, it's a social security number for your business. You can get a free EIN when you apply directly with the IRS.

I will get into more detail about registering your business in chapter three of this book to give you all the information you need.

Before you consider starting your vending machine business, it's good practice to check your state's regulations regarding vending. Each state could have different regulations depending on the type of product you are looking to sell from your vending machine. Products like milk products, soda, snacks, gumballs, candy, toys or capsules, and even tobacco products each have their own regulations depending on the state you are living in. The following regulations are for reference only; you should still check your state's ordinances to ensure you are up to date with regulations.

Florida: Venders are required to first have a license before they can start vending. This is important because they are selling products to consumers, and without a license, your business can be shut down, and you may receive a fine.

California: Venders need to have a seller's permit to place their vending machines. With one single permit, you are allowed to place as many machines as you prefer. There are however, certain restrictions, for example, if your products are less than 15 cents you need to acquire another permit. Another permit is needed for non-taxable vending machine sales.

Arizona: The federal government is actively working at reducing the number of children suffering from obesity, and for that reason, the regulations have become a lot tighter. They have also stopped the sale of foods with little to no nutritional value. Students are also restricted from accessing vending machines during lunchtimes, and vending machines placed in schools need to only offer 100% fruit juice or water.

Colorado: Owners, operators, and lessors of vending machines who have control over the receipts from their vending machines are required to obtain a tax license. The state of Colorado requires this license for you to run a vending business no matter how many machines you have or where they are located. Each machine should also have a decal.

Massachusetts: The state of Massachusetts requires owners to have a license issued by the commissioner to operate their business. This form should also have the signature of the applicant, otherwise it may not be valid. A label should also be placed on the machine with a license number that needs to be approved by the commissioner to be deemed valid.

You are required to know the regulations before you start your business, so when you are operational, you are doing it legally and within the state requirements.

One of the most important things to think about before starting your vending machine business is where you are planning to place your machines. Consider the following factors when deciding where you want to place your machines. The first thing to keep in mind is that your business needs customers to generate an income, and you need to consider the success of a business where you are planning to place your machine before contacting the business. Ask the following questions when considering a location:

• Are there locations in my area that require a vending machine? Manufacturing buildings? Retail stores? Elsewhere?

• What products should I sell in my vending machine? Candy, chips, soda, toys, or something else?

- Should my machine cater to workers on breaks or have more specialized products?

- How will I be able to get the perfect place with a specific location where I can place my vending machine?

After answering these questions, consider the area you are living in

When you determine the profitability of your vending machine, keep the following considerations in mind:

- **Accurate Identification of High-Revenue Locations:** You need to make sure that the location you are looking into will give you enough profit. These areas have high amounts of foot traffic, and this will ensure the success of your business.

- **Strategic Placement of Machines:** You need to ensure that you place your machines correctly within a location. For example, you wouldn't place it in a corner or corridor of a building where nobody passes through. Otherwise, the number of customers won't matter. Without customers, your business won't function properly, and this could mean your profit margins will take a dive, and you will not have enough money to cover any fixed expenses or generate a profit for your business.

The top locations to consider placing your machines include:

- **Laundromats:** Individuals who visit laundromats often give up an hour and a half of their time to wait for their laundry to wash and dry. This could lead them to want a snack or drink during this time. You may also want to consider placing machines that will dispense laundry detergent, fabric softener, or coin exchange. Arcade games are another possibility for your vending machines.

- **Offices and Commercial Properties:** Vending machines in an office building are utilized regularly by employees, especially during their breaks or lunch periods. You may want to do some research about what you think might sell according to the employee's liking and stock only those items. Healthy snacks and beverages are usually a good idea for these locations. Gyms and airports are also two great locations because they have limitless amounts of traffic that could increase your profit margin significantly.

- **Educational Institutions:** Students often look for snacks and drinks between their lecture halls or dormitories. Universities and high schools often work with big commercial organizations, but three are a few that will consider working with a smaller vendor.

- **Healthcare Facilities:** Institutions like hospitals, hospice centers, nursing homes, and outpatient medical facilities often have high foot traffic made up of practitioners and visitors. Especially patients will likely go to a vending machine to purchase snacks or beverages while waiting to be seen by a medical practitioner, depending on the waiting time. Placing your machines in spots like corridors like waiting rooms and break rooms will increase sales.

- **Residential Communities:** Apartment buildings often have common areas for their residents and use these areas to place their machines because they have a lot of traffic. These locations often have one or two machines near the recreational centers and exercise facilities. But you can inquire about placing machines near outdoor spaces should the location have a swimming pool or other outdoor activities for the residents.

• **Retail Locations:** Grocery stores, gas stations, liquor stores, and some major markets often have space for vending machines. Vending machines should be placed as close to the exits as possible to give clients access to the machines after they do their shopping.

The next important question you should be asking yourself before starting a vending machine business is what are you planning to sell to your audience. The variety of items individuals and businesses are selling in their machines has grown rapidly over the past few years, and many new items have started making their appearance in vending machines. I will discuss some of the most popular items sold below:

Food, Snack, and Beverages: Making up 86% of the vending market, this is possibly the obvious choice when you are looking to start your own vending machine business. One thing to keep in mind when you are going in this direction of supply is that your profit margin may be lower than with other products. Because these items are often bulkier, they may require restocking more often than others. Junk food is also more popular than healthier options unless you supply gyms and schools. Keep in mind that blue-collar workers often purchase more items from vending machines than white-collar workers, and men often purchase more than women.

Gumballs and Candy: These items will suit any location and are very popular in areas where there are a lot of children present. The mark-up related to this product is also higher than other items because you can sell a gumball for a 700% profit. They also require less restocking because these machines can hold thousands of items a once, and you will be able to take away a higher profit.

Cigarettes: Cigarette vending machines can hold a great amount of profit if they are placed in the right locations and you are aware of the regulations of your area.

Toys and Stickers: Placing vending machines holding these items in places like restaurants or shopping malls can bring you a high-profit margin. Since these vending machines hold a huge volume of items at once you will not be required to restock that often, and your return will be much higher.

Bathroom Related Products: These items have become more popular over the past few years because they are easily accessible to individuals who need them. Items like condoms, sanitary pads, fragrances, and soap will increase profit if placed in the right location. These items don't require regular restocking depending on usage and only require a small unit that is fixed to a wall.

The items you can provide through your vending machine are endless. All it takes is to pick the right item at the right time to give you a return on your investment. An example of this is vending machines selling masks and hand sanitizers to the public. This has become very lucrative and continues to grow. Starting with tried and tested products is your best road to success and will give you the knowledge and experience to continue growing your business with new and unique items.

The next thing you would need to consider if you want to succeed in the vending machine business is the purchasing of your supplies. The products you are looking at supplying to your audience need to be at the lowest cost possible to increase profit margins. You can get the products you are looking to supply at low cost from wholesalers, cash and carry suppliers, brokers of specialty products, or membership clubs. Choosing the right supplier is important to ensure success, and for that reason, I will discuss the different options below:

Wholesaler Pros: Wholesalers often offer between 1,000 and 50,000 different items that you can choose from in different sizes, from regular-sized products to king-sized and more. You can get anything you are looking to sell through a wholesaler in your area. Wholesalers often ship quicker than your regular grocery store due to the massive amounts of stock they have on hand, and your waiting wait will be between 24-48 hours should you need to restock machines fast.

Wholesaler Cons: One drawback of wholesalers is that shipping may become expensive and additional fees may be charged for smaller quantities. You need to consider these factors when it comes to your profit so that you are not spending more than you are earning. You would need to have quite a few machines to make use of wholesalers, because should you only have a few machines, you might be overbuying and not have the opportunity to supply the goods purchased before their sell-by date.

Cash and Carry Suppliers Pros: Cash and carry suppliers are often associated with wholesale distributors. They offer caseloads of particular items you can supply through your vending machines by ordering them and then picking them up at one of their locations. They offer the same products as wholesalers, and you can buy them in smaller quantities. Many also offer same-day pick up, which makes it convenient for you to service your vending machines on time.

Cash And Carry Suppliers Cons: When you stay far from your local cash and carry, it may not make sense to make use of these shops because your drive time and gas costs may dig into your profits. The price may also increase due to smaller quantities because smaller quantities require more packaging time, material, and manpower than caseloads of products.

Broker of Specialty Products Pros: These brokers offer recommendations for popular products and where you can purchase them, although some of them already work with some of your competitors. They can also purchase some of the products on your behalf and distribute them at a lower cost. These brokers can be very valuable, especially for beginners in the vending machine industry, because they give invaluable advice. They also negotiate with manufacturers so you can receive bulk discounts or rebates on larger quantities.

Broker of Specialty Products Cons: Most of these brokers prefer to work with established vending machine business owners with larger budgets and a bigger workload. You may be assigned with a junior broker when you use a broker for your start-up business and this could lead to fewer contacts and sources. These brokers may also be associated with a particular brand name of food, beverages, and other products, and this may be their primary sales force. You may need to find out which products your selected broker is associated with before partnering with them because they will be less likely to work with your best interests at heart if they do, especially when being paid commission.

Membership Clubs Pros: Costco, Sam's Club, and BJ's often offer membership clubs to vending machine business owners. These shops are often very similar to cash and carry suppliers, and they are perfect when you use them for quick restocks. Membership clubs also don't put massive mark-ups on the items they buy from wholesalers, and these prices are then passed on to you. This allows your business to sell products at the same price, and you will keep your profit margins steady. These shops are also conveniently close to your location, and you will be able to access one along your vending route and restock on items that sell out quickly. This cuts down on travel costs and time, which helps keep your profits high. The biggest benefit of membership clubs is the fact that you can return unused items for a full refund, whereas wholesalers will charge you a return and restocking fee.

Membership Clubs Cons: Membership clubs often have an annual fee you need to pay to gain access to the clubs - these are usually around $50 per year, depending on the club. These clubs may not always offer the same products every time you go to restock, which could mess around with your business.

The best way to find out how many existing vending machines are in your area is by doing your research and taking a look around your neighborhood. This will need to be done before you start your business to ensure that the competition is not too dense for you to enter the market. You can hire a professional broker to do the research for you and find locations on your behalf, but you would need to be cautious when attempting this route because this will open up an opportunity for scammers to take advantage of you.

The amount of time you would need to run your business depends on the effort you are willing to put into your business. Any start-up business takes a significant amount of effort to get off the ground, and this means that you would need to invest time to get your business running. There is no specific amount of time as this will depend solely on yourself. Keep in mind that the more time and effort you invest in your business - the faster you will get it operating.

You might now be wondering how many vending machines you would need. The fact is, this will depend on your business and the vision you have for it. You can start with as little as one machine and increase the number of machines you have as your business grows. Another thing you may want to keep in mind is the area you are aiming to service with your machines. The more locations you can obtain within your business, the more machines you would need to purchase to satisfy your clients.

The next thing you would need to focus on is finding locations for your vending machines. The first way you can do this is by doing your research regarding businesses in your area. There are a few apps and websites you can use to achieve this; data-axle is one of the most powerful tools to use when you start a vending machine business because you can filter your searches. You can search through locations, years of operation, number of employees, etc. Once you have found potential clients, it's time to get yourself out there and let these businesses know you are there and that you would like to partner with them. You may need to speak to a manager or owner of the company to get your vending machines placed. You also need to dress the part to show that you are professional and serious about your offer. Don't feel discouraged when the business already has a vending machine because you might have an opportunity to replace the existing machine. Especially when their machines are old and only sell junk food, you can offer a new high quality, customized vending machine accepting mobile payments, credit cards, and cash and contains healthier options to employees. Another effective way of getting locations is making every activity an opportunity to market your business. This means that for every location you visit, you can introduce yourself to the manager/owner and mention that you are looking for locations. These opportunities might just be what you need to gain the best locations for your machines, especially if you already know the people you are speaking to. Ensure that your friends and family know about your business because they might be able to provide you with opportunities at the companies they are working for. Below is a list of possible locations you can approach to place your vending machines:

- Airport

- Amusement park
- Apartment building
- Assisted living center
- Auto brake shop
- Auto dealership
- Bank
- Bingo hall
- Bookstore
- Bowling alley
- Bus station
- Business office building
- Car wash
- College/University
- Community Center
- Community swimming pool
- Computer store
- Dental office
- Department store
- Doctor's office
- Dormitory
- Driver's license division
- Dry cleaner
- Fire station

- Fraternity/Sorority
- Furniture store
- Gift Shop
- Golf course lounge
- Government office
- Gym
- Health club
- Hospital
- Hotel
- Humane society
- Ice skating rink
- Industrial park
- Laundromat
- Library
- Mall
- Manufacturing plant
- Medical building
- Meeting hall
- Military reserve/Guard center
- Military enlistment office
- Military treatment facility
- Miniature golf
- Motel

- Motor vehicle division
- Motorcycle shop
- Muffler shop
- Night club
- Nursing home/Retirement home
- Oil and lube center
- Police station
- Private school
- Public utility office
- Railroad station
- Recreation center
- Rental yard
- Rest stop facility (off Highway)
- Roller skating rink
- School
- Senior center
- Shopping center
- Ski Resort
- Stock brokerage
- Telemarketing office
- Tire store
- Tourist attraction
- Truckstop

- Trucking company
- Veteran's affairs facility
- Veterinary office
- Waiting room (any kind)
- Warehouse
- YMCA
- Youth center
- Zoo

Finding the perfect location is not rocket science but possibly one of the most overlooked aspects of this business model. The difference between a good and bad vending location is often the amount of foot traffic found in the location. The less traffic a location has, the lower your profit will be; you might incur a loss due to stock that needs to be tossed due to products being passed their expiration. A good vending location is one with a huge amount of foot traffic which means your profit margins will be higher, and products will be sold faster.

As a start-up vending machine business owner, there are some terms you would need to be familiar with to start your business. Below I will discuss some of the most important terms to remember:

- **Acceptor:** This is the mechanism that most if not all vending machines use to recognize the type of coin that is being placed in the vending machine.

- **Air Compressor:** Many vending machines have an air compressor built-in to keep items like sodas cold.

- **Bank of Equipment:** A-line with more than one vending machine.

- **Bill Validator:** Bill validators are mechanisms built into vending machines to validate the bills individuals use when purchasing items. They were installed in 1970 because more individuals started using bills instead of coins.

- **Broker:** An individual or company selling food and beverage products to vending machine owners.

- **Bulk Vending Machines:** These vending machines can dispense almost any items and often have glass fronts. They are also coin-operated and do not accept dollar bills.

- **C-Store:** Shortened term for convenience store

- **Category Management:** Managing your products sold from your vending machine, categorized. This means items are sorted together, for example, candies in one row and chips in another. Some machines may have 11 categories.

- **Changer:** A vending machine providing change without having to purchase an item.

- **Circuit Board:** A board located within the vending machine that controls the electronic mechanisms.

- **Cleaning Card:** A card that cleans bill validators.

- **Coin Mechanism:** The mechanism that dispenses and counts coins.

- **Coin-Op:** Shortened term for Coin Operated.

- **Cold Food Merchandiser:** A vending machine dispensing only cold foods.

- **Commissions:** A percentage of the revenue paid to the manager of a location by the vending machine owner.

- **Contract Vending:** When a contract is drafted between the vending machine owner and location manager for the installation and operational services of the vending machines.

- **Conversion Kits:** Changes amusement games using the same unit.

- **Cylinder Lock:** A lock used to open and close the door of the vending machine byways of sliding in and out of the machine.

- **Dispensers:** Machines that vend products.

- **Distributor:** A middle man between consumers and manufacturers.

- **Dolly:** Equipment used to move vending machines.

- **Equipment Distributor:** A company selling equipment and parts to vendors. They also offer new equipment training, maintenance and repair, and financing.

- **Food Service:** Only provides food services.

- **Forced Vend:** When an individual is forced to purchase a product before receiving change.

- **Free Vend:** When a machine is set so you can purchase products for free.

- **Full Line:** A full line of a variety of vending machines including snacks, drinks, coffee, and food.

- **Full Line Vendor:** A vending machine business owner offering vending machines dispensing different products.

- **Four C Vendor:** Cold drinks, coffee, candy and snacks, and cigarettes.

- **Gross Income:** The money collected from machines before expenses like commissions and taxes.

- **Installation:** Placing of vending equipment at set locations.

- **Jackpotting:** This is a term used within the vending industry for when cash is dispensed or products are given for free.

- **Kick Plate:** A front base cover for a vending machine.

- **Kiosk:** A small structure used as a newsstand, refreshment stand, etc.

- **Knockout:** A vending machine with a dollar bill acceptor installed.

- **LED Legs:** Leveling devices found at the bottom of the vending machines.

- **Lexan:** Front plate or panel advertisement on a machine.

- **Location:** A location with a machine installed or has space for a vending machine.

- **Manual Foodservice:** A machine offering conventional cafeteria or table service where customers can be served by people.

- **Manufacturer:** A company producing vending machines, products, coin and currency validating devices, and other equipment used by vending machine owners.

- **Mixed Route:** A route consisting of several different products and machines.

- **Music and Game Operators:** Companies providing video games, pinball, pool tables, cranes, and jukebox machines.

- **NAMA:** NAMA is the national trade association of the food and refreshment, coffee, and foodservice management industries.

- **National Vending:** This is a reference used to describe a company that services multiple areas regardless of its geographic location. These companies often have expert knowledge enabling seamless vending machine installations.

- **Net:** The profit received after expenses.

- **OCS:** Office Coffee Service. A company offering only coffee services.

- **Operator:** A vending machine business owner.

- **Par:** The number of items you may need to fill your machines.

- **Pour-Over:** A term used to describe a coffee machine where water is poured into the top of the machine.

- **Product Mix:** When a variety of products is vented from one machine.

- **Redemption:** A machine dispensing tickets that can be redeemed for products.

- **Route:** A set of locations where machines are placed. Different buildings or sites with machines installed in them.

- **Route Technician:** An individual who refills and services installed machines.

- Satellite Location: When a site is removed from the main location but is serviced by the same operator.

- **Shelf Life:** The time frame before a product expires.

- **Smart Card:** A card used with amusement game rooms, or breakrooms. Money is transferred to these cards and used in machines, similar to debit cards.

- **Token:** A specialized coin to use in some machines.

- **Token Dispenser:** A machine that exchanges money for tokens.

- **Truck Lift:** A mechanism at the back of a truck used to lift vending machines.

- **Validator:** A machine that accepts dollar bills and registers credit on vending machines. After the item is purchased, it will dispense the correct amount of change.

- **Vend:** To sell products using a vending machine.

- **Vend Cycle:** The timeframe a machine uses to vend one product.

- **Vending Brokerage:** A company representing a certain supplier that contacts operators and introduces new items, special promotions, gain information on specific items, and take orders.

- **Vending Cart:** A cart used for products to relocate them easily.

- **Vending Machine:** A machine that vends certain products.

- **Vending Operator:** An individual who owns a variety of vending machines at different locations and stocks them with products, services the machines, and collects money.

- **Wholesaler:** A company selling products for less than retail costs by buying directly from the manufacturer.

- **Yield:** When a high profit is received from products.

So owning a vending machine business might not sound profitable right now. But you will be able to quit your day job when you have the established route with several machines. So how many machines would you need to quit your day job and run your business full-time? Below is an example of what you need to earn a steady stream of income:

Number of machines: 10

Products vended per day: 25

Cost of each item: $0.50

The selling price of each item: $1.00

By using the numbers provided above, you will receive the following returns:

Daily Gross Profit: $125.00

Weekly Gross Profit: $625.00

Monthly Gross Profit: $2,500.00

Yearly Gross Profit: $32,500.00

Now let's use the following amounts:

Number of machines: 15

Products vended per day: 30

Cost of each item: $0.80

The selling price of each item: is $1.50

Using the above amount, you will receive the following profits:

Daily Gross Profit: $315.00

Weekly Gross Profit: $1,575.00

Monthly Gross Profit: $6,300.00

Yearly Gross Profit: $81,900.00

Keep in mind that these are simply estimated, and you would need to do some research to determine what you will be able to make.

You can do this by using the following formula:

Selling price - Purchase price = Profit

Profit x Units sold = Total received from one machine

Profits received from one machine x Number of machines = Total profit

Weekly gross profit = Total profit x 7

Monthly gross profit = Total profit x 30

Yearly gross profit = Total profit x 365

This formula will give you an estimate of how much you could receive from your vending machine business.

Chapter 3:
Opening Your LLC & Getting Your Equipment

When considering opening your own vending machine business, you might be wondering whether you should buy a new or used vending machine to start with. I will discuss some of the benefits and drawbacks of purchasing both new and used vending machines.

Benefits of purchasing a new vending machine:

- New vending machines can be financed.

- New machines often have built-in credit card readers and the latest processing technology.

- You will have a manufacturer warranty.

- They are location ready, so you won't be surprised by broken wires or worn tracks.

- Older machines are replaced with newer versions.

- They pay for themselves over time.

- You can gain the best traffic locations because you have the newest machines.

- Most locations prefer new machines since they are more profitable, durable, and last longer.

Advantages and disadvantages of buying used vending machines:

Assessing Machine Quality: You would need to ensure the machine is in working condition and if the machine has been refurbished and tested. Your customers are going to require functionality above everything else.

Cost Savings: Before purchasing a used machine, look at the clients you want to contact. Would they prefer a shiny new machine, or would they be happy with a used machine? You may be able to secure better locations (high-end gyms as an example) with a new machine as opposed to a used unit.

Terms of Agreement: Depending on the agreement you have with a client, you may need to be able to assure your client that the machines you provide will last for the length of your agreement.

Flexibility and variety: Purchasing a used machine can offer flexibility because a used machine's purchase price is often 20-30% lower than a new machine. This often means you would have more funds available to contribute to other areas of your business.

Sourcing your equipment is important when you start a vending machine business, and so is knowing how much you will need to pay for each type of machine. The price you would pay on machines depends on whether you purchase new or used machines. Below are the seven top websites I reccomend buying vending machines from, including their price range regarding vending machine type:

UsedVending.com: This website is used by most vending machine business owners because it gives you the option to search for products based on price, location, and type of vending machine you need. Known as a third-party website because it connects a seller with a buyer.

Some of the products listed on this website are as follows:

Used

- Combo Machines: $1,500 - $4,000
- Drink Machines: $1,000 - $4,000
- Snack Machines: $1,000 - $4,000

New

- Combo Machines: $3,500 - $5,000
- Drink Machines: $3,500 - $5,000
- Snack Machines: $3,500 - $5,000

Refurbished

- Combo Machines: $2,000 - $4,000
- Snack Machines: $2,000 - $4,000
- Soda Machines: $1,000 - $3,000
- Coffee Machines: $2,000 - $5,000
- Frozen Food Machines: $2,000 - $4,000

CraigsList.org: Although this site might not always have vending machines available, you might be able to snag a good deal when they do. You might need a little more patience when using this site as it does take a bit longer to search for products, but it will be well worth the effort.

Sam's Club: Offering the generic version of soda and snacks machines, you can buy entry-level vending machines from shops like Sam's Club. One benefit of buying from this retailer is the return on the equipment, and they offer free shipping to your home. You can expect to pay the following according to machine type:

- Snack Machines: $3,500 - $6,000
- Combo Machines: $3,000 - $5,000
- Soda Machines: $5,000 - $6,000

CandyMachines.com: This site sells only new machines dispensing items like gumballs, peanuts, and other smaller items like temporary tattoos. You can expect to pay the following according to the various machine types:

- Three head gumball and candy machines: $100 - $300
- Two-head gumball machines: $100 - $300
- Single-head candy machines: $100 - $200
- Crane vending machines: $900 - $4,000
- Combo Machines: $3,000 - $6,500
- Snack Machines: $4,000 - $6,000
- Soda Machines: $4,000 - $6,000
- Fresh Food: +- $5,500
- Frozen Food: +- $8,000
- Coffee: $2,500 - $3,500

eBay/Amazon.com: When using these sites, you will be able to see what previous buyers have to say regarding certain products. Although one thing you need to look out for, especially when purchasing gumball machines, is the quality. Some of these machines would work perfectly in a home environment but not necessarily for business purposes.

When deciding to purchase either a coin/cash operated vending machine or a cashless machine, there are many variables to consider. According to our experience, some of the most important tips to keep in mind are:

• Due to the change of lifestyle, fewer people are carrying cash these days, with many carrying less than $50 in their wallets. Up to 9% of people don't carry cash at all. Consumers prefer to pay with their debit or credit cards due to the convenience it brings.

• The newer generation of Americans say that they are comfortable being without cash and feel that being cashless is the future of society. Gen Z use their phones for almost everything, and with banks offering apps and virtual cards, it makes sense to offer cashless vending machines.

• Cashless machines will increase your profit because consumers will find it more convenient to pay with their debit/credit cards than with cash. Cashless machines will also increase customer satisfaction. Cashless machines may also speed up the process of balancing your company's books because you will not have to count all the cash before going to the bank.

- Impulse and convenience are major drivers for consumers, and for that reason, profits will increase when you use a card machine as individuals will be more prone to impulse buy at your vending machines.

- You can encourage your customers to use the cashless method by installing card readers on all your vending machines. You may also want to consider removing any means of cash payments from your vending machines to prevent the use of cash at your vending machines.

- There are a few cashless payment methods, including Android Pay and Apple Pay. Ensuring that your vending machines can accept this payment could prevent you from missing out on sales. This is because individuals often forget their wallets but very few forget their phones, and should you enable these features, individuals will have access to paying with their phones creating even more convenience as they will not have to go back and get their wallets to make use of your vending machines.

Purchasing the most expensive vending machines on the market will not save you the effort of having to fix them. You must make sure you purchase the best and most reliable machines on the market. For that reason, let's have a look at what a good quality machine should feature:

- **Low cost:** Unmanned vending machines typically cost a few thousand dollars. This makes it ideal for small business owners looking at leveraging the power of technology with a tight budget and limited capital.

- **Maintenance:** Machines need to be easy to maintain to be classified as one of the best; they need to eliminate complications with maintenance.

- **Efficiency:** Different machines have different functions, and for a machine to be classified as the best, it needs to be easy for the customer and owner to operate.

- **Flexibility:** Machines that can be placed in any location, including shopping centers, malls, supermarkets, schools, campuses, squares, airports, and tourist attractions, are deemed the best.

- **Compartments:** Machines that don't require frequent restocking because they can hold a significant amount of products due to big compartments are often the best way to go to ensure profitability.

- **Corrosive Resistant:** Vending machines companies have taken a step forward by creating machines that have corrosive-resistant shelves to eliminate this problem that business owners have.

- **Durable and Energy Saving:** Durability in a vending machine is important because the machine will be used by a variety of individuals. The machine would need to withstand the occasion when one of these individuals might be a bit rough. They also need an energy-saving design that will reduce your energy bill over time.

- **Alarm:** Some of the best vending machines already have this feature installed which protects the business owner against possibilities of theft and burglary, especially in public places.

Now that you know what features to keep in mind when purchasing your vending machines, I will get into some of the best vending machines that you can buy for your business:

• **Triple Pod Candy Vending Machine:** These machines have a very durable design and a big holding capacity, meaning you would not need to refill the machine quite so often. It is also very flexible because it can be placed at any location and has the basic features, including a drop-through coin process.

• **Kitna 45" Vending Machine:** These machines have a top-quality build with bulky compartments, extending their frequent refilling demand, and a powerful compressor ensuring products are kept cold. It also consists of an LCD monitor allowing easy control and observation of the temperature and shelves that are corrosive resistant.

• **AB 40/395 Food and Beverage Vending Machine:** Classified as possibly one of the best vending machines, it can hold sodas, beverages, candies, snacks, and dairy products. It has moveable barriers that allow you to control the temperatures that regulate through the machine, which means that different areas have different temperatures according to the products you are stocking. This model also has a built-in alarm system and is rated as having efficient energy consumption. **This is our favourite machine.**

• **SEAGA Vending Machine:** A tried and tested vending machine with the option to provide over 40 different products. These vending machines allow you to provide both edible and non-edible products all in one machine. It has LED lighting, which makes it attractive to look at - and also has a scroll pricing feature that makes it convenient for consumers to use.

Other than the vending machines, you need to ensure that you have the following in place before starting your vending machine business. You would need to apply for permits and ensure you have all the licenses, certificates, and insurance requirements that are needed in place. Once your business license is in place, you must apply for the right to sell food items. Both the vending machine business owner and the owner/manager of the location in which the vending machine is placed should have a food vending machine license obtained from their local Department of Consumer and Regulatory Affairs. Certain states are exempt from these licenses if the machine sells pre-packaged, non-perishable foods or bottled/canned, non-perishable drinks and gumball machines. A complete application for a basic business license for the food vending machine category includes the following items:

- Corporate registration
- Tax registration
- Certificate of occupancy
- List of vending machines
- List of foods you will be selling
- Application tax paid

The taxes that you may need to pay will vary depending on your state. But the following fees may be included:

- Category license fee
- Application fee
- Endorsement fee
- Technology fee

These fees may also be charged per unit, and the license duration is often two years. The following items may not need a vending machine license:

- Cigarettes
- Magazines
- Newspapers
- Paper cups
- Paper or cloth towels
- Postage stamps
- Sanitary napkins
- Soap and toilet seat covers

When starting your vending machine business, it is safer to only purchase the number of products that will fit inside. This is because you will have a better opportunity to see which products are popular and which are not, preventing you from sitting with products that may expire. You may also want to consider asking people that use your vending machine which products they would like you to stock so you can supply products that will sell. Overstocking items is never a good idea as you might end up with expired goods that could cost you your profit over time. You will need to throw these items away once they expire.

Now, let's look at how to register your business as an LLC. Starting an LLC is not as expensive or difficult as you might imagine. We will be covering everything you need to know regarding how to register your business, how much it costs, how long it takes, where you need to do it, and the documents you will need below.

The first thing you would need to do when you want to register your business is to choose the state you want to operate in. Forming an LLC in your home state is cheaper, faster, and will be more convenient for you.

The next thing you need to do is choose a name for your LLC. You might find this step to be quite daunting and you may not know what to name your business. You can choose an easy name for your business. As your business grows and the name does not seem logical anymore, you can apply for a DBA and set up a trading name for your business. When you own a trading name, your business will have rights to a fictitious business name. Your business name does, however, still need to follow your state's naming requirements. Once your name is set up, you can start designing new flyers, mailers, a website, and contracts.

The following requirements for naming your business are universal, but I do suggest you follow up with your state to ensure you don't need anything else:

- Unique name

- The name must include the phrase "Limited Liability Company," "LLC," or "Ltd."

- Your name should not include confusing phrases like "IRS," "Department of State," "Police Department," etc.

- Words that are protected should also be left out of your name; these include "College," "Hospital," or "Bank."

Once your business name is set up, and your business is running under an LLC, you should look into appointing a registered agent for your business. Any person 18 years or older can be appointed as your registered agent as long as they have a physical address in the state in which your LLC has been formed. You can also appoint yourself as a registered agent for your company, although I would advise you against that. A registered agent is publicly accessible, so if you appreciate your privacy it would be best to appoint another registered agent. Registered agents often don't take vacations, don't take sick days, and never leave the office during regular business hours. Legal papers get sent to your business's registered agent and should you miss a legal document due to being absent it may cost you your business. Registered agent companies often charge $120 per year and attorneys could charge up to $500 per year, for that reason, you may consider appointing a company that has dedicated registered agents to handle legal documents on your behalf.

The next step will be to file your articles of organization with your Secretary of state. This will form your limited liability company. In some states, they are known as a certificate of formation or certificate of organization. The documents that you would need to submit, include:

- Your business address
- Name and address of your registered agent
- Name and address of your founding members
- Whether your business is managed by members or non-member managers
- Effective date
- Duration of your LLC
- Business purpose statement

Submitting these documents can be done via email or online, and the filing fee will depend on your state. Formation services often file these documents for free when you purchase their formation packages, and they also ensure all the information provided is free of errors. These services complete the entire process of formatting and incorporating an LLC on behalf of the business; they are often the fastest and easiest option to choose. They are also more affordable than lawyers or a CPA because they work online.

Your second last step is to create an operating agreement. This is possibly the most important document in your company because it sets the rules of how your company works internally and how it will work with the public. Although you might not require one depending on the state you form your LLC, it is good practice to have one set up at the start of your business. With this document in place, your assets like houses, cars, and savings accounts are saved should you be sued or your business goes bankrupt. Operating agreements make sure that the following protections are in place:

- The operating agreement should state the rights and responsibilities of each member within the LLC.

- The agreement should state the rights and responsibilities of all non-member managers within the LLC.

- The operating agreement should clearly state what the business will be doing on a day-to-day basis, and the business it will be conducting.

- Set rules should be mentioned in the agreement on how new members will be able to join and how existing members can leave the business.

- It should also say how and when profits will be paid over to members of the business.

- State whether members or managers have authority within the company and how they intend to hire or fire managers.

- You might want to think about how you would close your company when the time comes to ensure it doesn't become an issue. This should also be stated in your operating agreement.

- You should also include rules for changing your operating agreement, for future use.

Finally, get an EIN (Employer Identification Number). This number is the nine-digit tax identification number for your business. The IRS uses this number to track your business entities for tax purposes. This number is a requirement for any business generating revenue. It is also required by some banks when you apply to open a business bank account. This number is obtained through the IRS and can be done online, or you can submit a form SS-5 via post. This number is available immediately when applying online.

Although there are many business structures available when you want to start your vending machine business, you would need to know which one is the best. Below I will be explaining the different kinds of business structures and how they work so that you can have a better understanding of each of them:

Sole Proprietorship: These business structures are easy to set up and cost very little to start. Their profits can also easily be drawn into financial affairs without trouble. Although this might sound attractive, you need to look at the negative aspects of the business as well.

Sole proprietorships are adjunct to yourself, meaning all the legal and financial responsibilities of the company fall directly on you. In other words, the company is directly linked to yourself as a person and not as an independent entity. Registering your business under a Sole Proprietorship means you will be personally responsible for any credit that the company has, and banks can take your car, house, or other property should you lapse on these payments. Another negative of this business structure is that should you pass away, the business perishes with you, and this means you will not be able to pass the company on to your children.

C-Corporations: This type of business structure could work for a vending company, but you would need to remember that this structure is best for bigger companies or companies that intend to grow. The structure has quite costly licensing, legal requirements, and administrative costs linked to it, and for that reason, it is not the best option for start-up companies. With smaller companies often having smaller profits, you might not want to be taxed twice for the same amount of money. One positive aspect of this business structure is that no one will have access to your finances or property, and legal action is taken against the corporation and not against yourself.

S-Corporations: S-corporations and C-corporations are very similar; the only main difference is that C-corp structures are considered to be "pass-through" entities. This means that any funds earned from the operations the company provides become the property of the business owner instead of the business itself.

Limited Liability Company (LLC): An LLC business structure is the most favorable for the vending machine business because your assets and property, just like an S-Corp, are protected in case of legal action. Another similarity is that profits become personal income instead of business income. Setting up an LLC is also very user-friendly and more flexible than corporations. The only thing you will need is an operating agreement to maintain the status of your LLC. Limited liability companies have to remit taxes based on their undistributed profits, and both the owner and partners will be responsible for filing their income taxes. Some other benefits of registering your company as an LLC are that it is informal, flexible, scalable, and provides you with sufficient legal and tax protection.

The directors of an LLC are often referred to as members of an LLC, they are typically responsible for the day-to-day running of the business. The main responsibilities of an LLC manager are to ensure that personal and business finances are kept separate at all times. This can be done by the following:

- Setting up a business bank account and keeping business and personal funds separate.

- Sign business documents as an officer or member of the business.

- Including the letters "LLC" after the name of the business name on all corresponding documents, invoices, business cards, and other documents the company might distribute.

LLCs also have a different way of paying their members and handling taxes, and it is the manager's responsibility that taxes are handled appropriately. Some of the other day to day responsibilities of an LLC manager are:

- **Management:** Manage the business every day

- **Money:** Accounting and financial management

- **Marketing and sales:** Management of sales, marketing, and customer service

- **People:** Manage the productivity of employees as well as training and developing skills of employees

- **Product and service:** Keeping up with day to day operations, managing quality and quantity, price, display, stock, and distribution of products

- **Process and systems:** Keeping up with daily processes and systems like admin and bookkeeping

Other responsibilities of business owners include contributing to society and developing skills to become a valuable business asset in your area. You also need to strengthen the business inside so you can expand on the outside. Define your mission, goals, and visions for your company. Keep control of all your business finances and focus on the fundamentals of your business, like making money and generating an income. Improve your bottom line and maximize your long-term profitability. You need to build a unique business model that builds customer loyalty and trust, and you should continue to innovate on your products which will add value and improve the quality and quantity of the service you offer. Expanding your business to the outside world would require that you defend and maximize your market and wallet share. Focus on financial strategies and identify your source of funds. Make investments that build your company assets and overall long-term worth. Exploiting your existing resources and developing the resources you need. Spotting trends and opportunities and eliminating any threats or weaknesses that may present themselves. Develop advantages in established markets to eliminate the increase in competition. Some of the financial responsibilities of a business owner include daily bookkeeping like creating invoices, delivery notes, updating customer details, handling accounts receivables and payable, and overall keeping the accounting system up to date.

The next thing you would want to do with your vending machine business is to join NAMA (National Automatic Machine Association). There are a members benefits when you join the association, including:

- Enjoying the benefits of advocacy work at all levels of the government.

- Staying up to date with regulatory issues that have an impact on the industry.

- Development of relationships with influential lawmakers on capitol hill.

- Gaining experience as an advocate for the industry.

- Engaging in grassroots efforts to fight legislation and unfair taxation.

- Learning to improve your operation and gain industry knowledge.

- Tapping into industry news, trends, and innovations.

- Making informed decisions based on research, including the industry census and economic impact study.

- Consultation with knowledgeable source partners.

- Receiving discounts on registration fees for webinars, the NAMA show, and coffee, tea, and water shows.

- Secure special deals on shipping, travel, and more.

- Purchase publications at a significantly discounted rate.

- Growing your business and advancing your career by attending timely and relevant pre-conference workshops and education sessions.

- Advance your career and business with personalized development.

- Becoming an expert in your field by taking advantage of online courses and webinars.

- You can build and strengthen relationships with colleagues and industry leaders.

- Join member communities where you get to engage with peers and share ideas.

- Rely on staff that will work with you.

You can join the NAMA community by visiting their website and creating a new account. You can also ask any questions that you might have by emailing or calling them at members@namanow.org or 888.337.8363.

Choosing a name for your vending machine business might seem daunting, but following these steps can make the process so much easier for you.

- What will your business be doing? You may want to review your mission statement, your business plan, and your selling proposition. Consider your target audience and the research you have done on the market when considering your business name. Ask yourself the following questions when you are deciding on your business name:

- What is the message that you want to send to your customers?

- What are the major priorities of your business name? Would you like your name to be easy to pronounce, different and unique, directly related to the services you are aiming to offer?

- What should clients think or feel when they see the name of your business?

- Will your business name contain an abbreviation like LLC?

- Research the names of your competitors. What do you like or dislike about them?

- How long should your business name be?

• Conduct a few brainstorming sessions and try to determine what you should name your business. You will be surprised at what you can come up with when you start to think about it. You can create lists, mind maps, and word associations to help you determine your business name.

• Give it some time. Once you have all the possibilities written down, you can start narrowing down what you like and what won't work. You need to let your preconceptions and biased thoughts settle before you consider your business name. Choosing your business name is an important part of your business because it will represent your business and what services you will be offering. For that reason, you would need to sleep on your decision once you have a shortlist of potential names. Let the name you choose settle before making your final decision to ensure that it will fit your business.

- The next thing is to check the availability of the name you are choosing to use. You can do this by checking the federal database of the U.S. Patent and Trademark Offices. You should also search the name you choose on Google or other search engines to ensure the name is available. Should your business name not be available as a domain, then you can use abbreviations, hyphens, or a top-level domain, such as .net. You do, however have to consider how easy it will be for your clients to remember and use your domain to find your website. Not being clear on your domain name and what your clients have to add could mean that you will be losing them to your competitors.

- Register your business name. To secure your business name, you will want to register your business with state authority. You can also register your business name as a trademark, which further protects the name from being used by anyone else.

Choosing a business name could be a timely process, but it will be well worth the effort when you launch your business. You will look more professional, and your business will come across much better.

Once you have established and registered your business name, you'd want to create your very own logo for your vending machines. They are a great way of advertising your business and making yourself more visible to new potential customers. Logos can be added to your business documents, business cards, and advertisements, so clients will know what your business name is.

Now you can start creating business cards for your business to hand out to potential clients. You can decide to design your business cards and have them printed out, or you can opt for a professional to design business cards on your behalf and have them printed. These are seven top business card printing services available should you decide to design them yourself:

- Vistaprint
- Zazzle
- Elite Flyers
- PsPrint
- GotPrint
- MOO
- Staples

You can opt to get printed business apparel for your vending machine business to increase your marketing services. Branded clothing can increase the reach of your target audience. You would need to get individuals to wear your t-shirts to create visibility; by doing this, you can create walking advertisements for your business. The best t-shirt printing companies taking over the market currently are:

- Designhill
- Vistaprint

- UberPrints
- DiscountMugs
- Broken Arrow Wear
- CafePress
- Spreadshirt
- Custom Ink
- DesignAShirt
- TeeSpring
- Printful
- Printify
- Kite
- PrintAura
- Omaha Print Shop

When you start your vending machine business, you need to have your business phone number and voicemail set up so your customers can get in contact with you easily. With technology evolving, you can set up your business line using your cellphone to ensure you can get in contact with clients wherever you are. A business phone number plays a big role in your clients' first impression. You can inspire trust, encourage conversations, and show clients that your company is professional. There are a few different types of phone numbers you can choose from for your business. These include:

- 800 number for your business: Also referred to as a toll-free number. Toll-free numbers have a significant impact on your customer experience because they aren't tied to a specific location. Having a business number with this prefix can also tell your customers that you are an established brand.

- Local phone numbers: When you are planning on only working in a certain area, then you might want to obtain a local phone number instead.

- Paid services are typically more reliable than free services even though they might be a little expensive. You may want to research apps that can provide you with a second phone line.

Remember that the wrong number can negatively affect your customer's experience with your brand. You need to have a well-researched understanding of the services available before choosing. You can have a look at SmartLine when you are looking at service providers. They have features you can use to streamline communication with your customers, look professional, and help you stay organized.

- Choose a toll-free or local U.S. phone number
- Separate business calls from personal calls
- Set a customized voicemail greeting
- Set business hours
- Get voicemail on the goal.

Once you have obtained your business phone number, you need to set up a voicemail for your business, so your customers see the professionalism of your business. You can set a voicemail message with the help of

SmartLine or create one yourself. When you set up the voicemail for your business, you might want to avoid the following:

- Cliches like 'Your call is important to us' - this term doesn't feel sincere.
- Make your voicemail friendly and personal.
- Don't let your voicemail sound read.
- You can hire a voice artist to record your voicemail greetings.
- Include important information like your business name, hours, and contact information in your voicemail.

Example of voicemail recording

After hours voicemail greetings example:

'Hi, you've reached [business name]. We are available by phone from [time] to [time] [PST] Monday to Friday. You can also use the contact form on our website, [www.example.com] to leave us a message and we will get back to you via email. If you'd like us to call you back, then please leave your name and number after along with a short message, and our team will get back to you as soon as possible."

Vacation Voicemail Greeting Example:

"Hello, you've reached [business name]. Our team is currently out of the office to spend holidays with friends and family. We'll be back to work on [day and time]. Please leave us your name and number and we will get back to you as soon as possible. [Happy holidays (or greeting for that holiday)."

Away or Busy voicemail greeting example:

"Hi, you have reached [business name], we are unable to take your call right now but we would love to call you back as soon as possible. Please leave us your name and number after the beep."

You can now look at setting up a virtual business address to help your business look more professional. A virtual address is a real street address at a mail center or office building location where you want to receive mail and packages. A virtual office address can be set up with the help of iPostal1. With the use of this service, all your mail and packages will be received by professional staff, you will also be able to manage your mail from anywhere using an app or online platform. You can add additional addresses to make your business reach wider. You might be thinking why this is necessary, but the fact is if you want to expand your presence in a new market you need a virtual business address

Once everything else is set up you can start looking at the insurance needs for your business. Now you might be wondering what type of insurance you need for your business. There are a few different types of insurance that cover various situations; these include but are not limited to:

General Liability Insurance

This is possibly the most popular type of insurance taken by business owners, and covers the following:

- Bodily injury
- Property damage

- Medical payments
- Legal defense and judgment
- Personal and advertising injury

Although you might not need to carry general liability insurance, operating without it could be harmful to the future of your business. The cost of general liability insurance is often between $500 and $1,000 per year for $1 million in coverage. Your premium is determined by the following:

- Location
- Deductibles
- Number of employees
- Pre-occurrence limit
- General aggregate limit

Commercial property insurance: This type of insurance is required when you own the property you use to manufacture, house, or stock your vending machines. This insurance protects your inventory as well as repair or replace broken inventory caused by vandalism, bad weather, or fires.

Workers Compensation Insurance: When you have employees working in your business, you would need to consider getting this type of insurance to protect your employees from potential accidents or injury. The machines they work with are heavy and often difficult to maneuver, and this could safeguard them against any physical harm.

Commercial Auto Insurance: You would need this type of insurance when your company has vehicles to transport your machines.

Business Interruption Insurance: This type of insurance will safeguard your business in case your operation is interrupted for a specific reason like fire, bad weather, or criminal activity.

Product Liability Insurance: This insurance covers the business owner should a product cause physical injury to a client.

Other things you need to obtain along with your insurance policies are the required licenses and permits to operate in your state. These license fees vary depending on the municipality that you reside and operate in, so you would need to check with your local government to find out how much you would need to pay. After obtaining your license, you would need to place your license sticker on all your vending machines. The only special circumstances are when your products are sold for less than 15 cents.

Once you have all your licenses, permits, insurance, and registrations in place and you can finally start to introduce your vending machine business, you would need to consider if it would be better to first source clients or first purchase your machines. I would suggest that you first start sourcing your clients and get signed contracts before purchasing machines. This will help you not waste any money. This is because there is no guarantee that you will gain clients once your machines are available, and you might be sitting with assets that are taking up space and a hole in your bank account. Once you have signed contracts and you know exactly how many machines you need, you can go shopping and purchase the number of machines and stock needed to start earning passive income.

When looking at the vending machine industry, it's a better option to start from scratch because it will give you more flexibility, and you get to start with only a few machines and build from there. Another benefit of starting a vending machine business from scratch is that you will learn as you go. This allows you to grow with your business and build skills and experiences that are invaluable to your business. Buying an existing business could be riskier, especially when you don't have any experience in the business yet.

Chapter 4:
Negotiating With Local Businesses and Tactics For Securing Locations/Routes

I would like to thank you for taking the time to read this book, and would love if you will leave a five-star rating on amazon if you found it valuable.

This part of the book will address how you can reach out to local businesses and offer to rent or profit share a location for your vending machine. We have covered the best locations to place your vending machines at the beginning of this chapter. You can review it again to establish which location is the best. Next, you need to consider whether it is better to have a fixed rental or a profit share agreement? For example, when you profit split a location, your client/owner of the space will receive a % of your profits. With a fixed fee, your client/ owner of the space will receive a specific amount every month, regardless of how many products you sell. We will now cover each option's pros and cons so you can determine which option will work better for you.

Renting location space pros:

- Dedicated space, you will not be sharing the space with anyone else.

- You will receive rentals and leads from the owner of the rental space.

Renting office space cons:

- You will be paying a predetermined amount of money every month regardless of the income you receive every month.

- You will be less likely to get quality leads or referrals because the location owner will still receive their money regardless if you make money or not.

- Having to pay this fixed amount will hurt your overall cash flow.

I would suggest a profit share agreement, especially when starting your vending machine business, as you can negotiate the terms of this agreement. You can establish a sliding profit share agreement to start with, and this would look something like this:

- 1st 2 months 90/10
- 2nd 2 months 80/20
- 3rd 2 months 75/25
- Finally 70/30

The best way of going about this would be to ask your client if they will consider an 80/20 profit share, and if you are lucky they will accept, and you will not need to offer a sliding scale. To safeguard both yourself and the client, once you have settled on an agreement type, you would need to put pen to paper. This means you need to draft an agreement where both you and your client can sign on the dotted line.

Some of the locations that you will target will typically require a fixed fee. This could range from $5 for simple machines like gumball machines, to as much as $50 for coffee, snack, and soda machines that require electricity and water. Other locations will require a percentage of your profits, these percentages could range from 5% to 25%, depending on the machine's income.

Starting a vending machine business from scratch means you need to know how to approach location owners and how to get a meeting with them to introduce your business and services. The first thing you would need to do before approaching new clients is to do your homework, this prepares you for that first initial meeting, and you will be more confident and ready to answer any questions the client may have for you. You can follow the tips below to better your chances of getting access to a location:

Define your value proposition: You need to determine what makes your services better than others, as well as the competition currently located in the space. You need to determine what your competition is currently offering and if you will be able to improve on the services they are offering. You need to focus on providing a better service than your competitor. This is also known as your value proposition. You might want to include that you are offering a wider variety of snacks and sodas than your competitors. You can also mention that you offer card or digital payments instead of just accepting cash, should your machines accept them.

Emphasize the contrast: You can emphasize the value that your business will bring. You can do this by asking the following questions to your potential location manager:

'Tell me about your current situation.'

'What's not working right now?'

'What happens if you don't deal with this and find a solution?'

'And what is that going to cost you?'

You can incorporate these questions into your proposition to help reveal the solution you will provide to their problems.

Manage your behavior: You need to be mindful of how you start a conversation with your potential location owner. Some of the things you might want to avoid when talking to your clients are:

• Starting with how bad the traffic/weather is or how tired you are. It simply starts the conversation off on the wrong foot.

• Don't speak badly about the competitors you are trying to overtake. Gossiping about them could create mistrust, and this will undermine your credibility.

• Accentuate that you have extremely high expectations of the location manager; using superlatives to describe the client, the location, end-customer, etc., works in your favor. This is because people live up to positive labels.

• Watch your body language. When you use nonverbal communication, you can be so much more successful.

- End on a high note.

Once you have discussed everything with the client and you are close to closing the deal, then it's best not to be too pushy. Keep in mind that selling to existing locations is less beneficial to the bottom line of your company, but it does improve and streamline your operations. No, you need to maintain a healthy relationship with your clients by being proactive, requesting feedback for better offerings, and leveraging a vending management system. I will discuss these in more detail below:

Be proactive: Make sure that you call your location manager regularly. This can help you to upsell more machines as well as help you to determine if a shorter service cycle is needed. You should also consider changing up the products you offer, but you need to find out if they will sell.

Feedback: The best way to find out what your customers want is to ask them. In an industry where you have direct access to your customers, you can find out what they want by doing the following:

- Conduct a survey or poll from your customers
- Use social media and forums
- Conduct in-person conversations

Leveraging a vending management system: Using this system from the start of your business can help you to monitor your customer preference by taking a look at the most purchased items. You will also be able to keep your vending machines stocked up by tracking the levels of certain items and how you can reorder your machine per location. This system will also help you to build trust with your clients because they can see that you are dedicated to offering good customer service.

Chapter 5:
Operational Management, Security, and Profit Margins

"I got lucky because I never gave up the search. Are you quitting too soon? Or are you willing to pursue luck with a vengeance?"

Jill Konrath

Once your vending machine business is up and running and you start earning money from your machines, it's time to start collecting the coins/cash. You need to take out the dollar bills and coins, the necessary cash that you can place into your change fund. You then need to place the rest in your collection bags without mixing up the bill types if possible. This will make the counting of your profit go so much easier when the time comes. You can place your money in a ziplock back and place it where it will be saved while you are busy filling up your machine with the necessary products. You need to get the paper slip after collecting all the cash so you can see how card payments have been doing since you last collected any funds. You would want separate collection bags for each machine/location, so you don't confuse what profit you make from each different machine/location.

Depending on the types of machines you are placing in locations, you need to familiarize yourself with where you can collect your money. For example, with gumball machines, your profit will be located in a slot behind the machine, as with soda and vending machines, you need to open the door to the machine and find the collection boxes behind the door. You would also need to time your collection to increase your profitability. For example, you can check smaller machines like gumball machines once a month, whereas soda and snack machines can be checked once a week. For arcade machines like coin pushing machines, you can check them once every two weeks.

When you set up your machine at a location, you need to add change so your customers can get change when paying larger bills. You need to add the following to your machine to ensure your clients will get the change they need when purchasing products from your machines:

- 25 Nickels
- 25 Dimes
- 25 Quarters
- +- 10 one-dollar bills

These amounts are totally subjective according to how often your machines get used and how often you refill them to ensure your machine has the right change to provide to your clients. The best way to determine exactly how much change you need to place into your machine will be to check your locations regularly to see how much change you still have available.

Once your machine is operational, you may not need to carry change rolls with you as you can fill your change slots with the profits you collect from your machine.

Your next step will be to fill your machine with depleted products. You can go in when collecting your profits and then look at which slots are empty. You then need to return to your vehicle, get the products needed, and go back to fill your machine. Once you get a hang of your location and what products sell out quickly you can predict which items you will need and bring a cart in with you and refill your machines immediately after collecting your cash. When you start your vending machine business you can follow these easy steps when filling your vending machine:

- Open your machine and take the reading of your products

- Fix any problems the machine may have

- Collect all the cash and balance the change

- Fill the machine with depleted items

- Write down the products you don't have with you that need restocking

- Return to your vehicle and get everything else you may need

When you reach your machines, you would need to know where you can stop your vehicle to simplify the process as much as possible. You would need to park your car so you can easily have access to the back of your vehicle, you won't block traffic, you are as close to the location as possible, and your truck can get in and out easily. You also need to protect your frozen products from melting by stopping in a spot that doesn't have direct sunlight on your vehicle.

The frequency in which you need to check and restock your vending machine will depend on a variety of different factors, like foot traffic and the products that you intend to sell. I will discuss the most popular types of vending machines and how often you would need to check on them to ensure the best profitability for each.

The first machine you would need to consider is a cold food vending machine, these machines often need regular maintenance to ensure they are working properly, and should you place them in areas within hospitals or airports, then they may need more regular restocking. The other major issue with these types of machines is you need to ensure the food is as fresh as possible. So you would need to check these machines at least twice a week for maintenance and checking on items.

The next machine is the soda and snack machine. They may not need often check for maintenance or restocking as these items tend to last a while, but you will still need to check your machines at least once a week, especially to collect funds. You may want to chat with your location manager/owner to find out which product is selling the best so you can focus more on popular products and eliminate the products that are not so popular. These machines often have lower overheads and higher profit margins due to the lower maintenance they require.

The final vending machine type I will be addressing is a coffee machine. These machines need to be checked as often as possible, and this is because they would need regular restocking depending on the area they are located. In a busy office building, this machine may need to be restocked at least two times per week to ensure significant cups, lids, stirrers, and of course, coffee, is supplied.

Now that you have collected all your cash and coins and you have restocked your machines, you will need to work with the profit that you have collected from your machines. You can create rolls of coins that you can keep on hand when your machines need to be stocked, or you can deposit these coins at your local bank if they allow it. There is, however, another option when dealing with all the coins that you have collected, and this entails finding out if your bank does bulk coin deposits. Some banks allow this and they do provide bags for bulk coin deposits. Banks often don't have a problem with dollar deposits so you will be able to do this at the nearest branch of your preferred bank. When you do find a bank that accepts bulk coin deposits, you would need to get a scale so you can insert the number of coins allowed per coin bag so you won't be denied when you take the cash to the bank.

There are banks or credit unions that have coin-counting machines. However, you typically have to be a member of the bank to use these facilities. Non-members of a bank often have to pay a fee to use this service. The following banks will typically still accept your coins:

- Citibank (requires coins to be rolled and fees may vary)

- Community savings banks (requirements often vary)

- U.S. Bank (You don't have to roll your coins but this service is only available to members of the bank)

  - Bank of America (requires coins to be rolled)
  - First county bank
  - Western Credit Union
  - Peoples United

You need to phone your bank in advance to find out if they require your coins to be rolled or if you can bring them as is. You also need to find out if there are fees for being a member or non-member. Ensure that your coins are clean before taking them to the bank. Most banks accept all types of coins, and there is often no limit on the type of coin you can exchange, although again you would need to phone your bank to find out what they require.

Now that the issue of depositing your profits has been discussed, let's talk about how you need to price your items to make a significant profit. I will discuss a few real-life examples now:

- 20oz. Soda: Sodas of this size sell for between $1.50 and $2.00. A pack of 24 on Amazon sells for around $41.57, this means that your cost price will be $1.73 each. This means that you would rather want to pass on this product because the profit margin that you will receive is quite low.

- Skittles and Starburst: These popular candies are often sold at $1.50. A pack of 30 of these candies is currently sold at $24.99 at Costco. This means your cost on this product will be around $0.83 each. So when selling this product for $1.50, you would make a profit of $0.67

per item. With this profit margin, it's a clear choice to add this product to your vending machines.

You would preferably want to receive at least $1 profit on each item you sell or at least a 50% profit. But above all the profit margins you would need to consider the demand for products. Just because you can make a ton of money on a specific product does not necessarily mean it will sell at all your locations. So you need to look at what products your customers would like to buy, and then look at the pricing options. You would also need to be competitive especially when other vending machine businesses are close to where your machines are placed and how they are pricing their items to prevent the possibility of missing out on a sale because another machine is cheaper.

When it comes to increasing the prices of the products you sell in your vending machine you need to consider the products you are offering your clients. This means that the higher quality the product is that you are offering, the more you can sell it for. For that reason, you can offer higher quality products from time to time at higher profit margins to increase sales. With regards to your regular products, you can consider increasing your prices once a year depending on inflation and other price increases. You need to keep in mind that your vending machine is paying for all your other expenses related to running your business like gas, cell phone, and time spent. So when the fuel prices increase, it would make sense to increase your item prices but be mindful of how much you want to increase to prevent your clients from feeling they are being ripped off.

Now we will move on to the servicing and fixing of your vending machines. There are various things that can cause your machine to break, and you would need to know how to fix them quickly so you don't lose out on potential sales. I will discuss some of the smaller problems that you can fix yourself:

- **Jamming issues:** A simple solution to prevent this is to ensure that your vending machine is a few inches away from the wall to ensure the machine has enough ventilation and your drinks won't get frozen due to poor ventilation. You also must ensure that your vending machine thermostat is aruond least 35 to 40 degrees Fahrenheit.

- **Returning coins:** When your machine is returning coins to a client, then there are two possible causes. These causes are because the product is not available or there may be a jam in the machine. Should the product be available you would need to clear the jam that is causing coins to be returned. You also need to check that the wheels within the machine are working. These are the two most important checks when it comes to this issue.

- **Not taking bills:** There are two problems when your vending machine is refusing to take bills, these are because there isn't enough change available or your bill validator may be dysfunctional. You may need to replace your bill validator and test the machine to ensure it is working fine.

- **The machine heats up:** Check that your machine is not placed too close to the wall, so it has sufficient ventilation. You also need to check your thermostat and check if your cooling fan is working properly and that it is indeed cooling your machine.

• **Periodic checks:** There are small checks that you do now and again to check if your machine is indeed working properly. Doing smaller checks at shorter intervals could prevent big problems from happening in the future which can save you money, time, and unnecessary problems.

One problem many vending machine business owners often come across is how they can manage their stock properly. But managing your inventory properly can significantly boost your profits. You need to consider the following when you are managing your inventory:

• What kind of machines do you own?

• What products do you want to sell?

• How many machines do you have?

• How much product do the machines sell between refilling?

The type of machines you are placing in locations is important especially when it comes to managing your inventory. A quick example is soda machines will often sell out quicker than snack machines so they would need more regular refills. When looking at combo machines, they often need more refills than any of the above because clients will have the opportunity to buy a snack and drink in the same location.

Now let's discuss the topic of selling the most successful products in your vending machine. Your first step will be to find out which products are selling out quicker than the rest. Once you define which products are the most successful you can focus on making sure your machine is always stocked with these items. The more these items are available to clients, the more they will be willing to purchase these items, and in the end, you will receive a higher profit margin. Another effective way is converting your machines to allow them to accept more payment methods. When customers see that your vending machines accept credit/debit cards they will be more willing to purchase items from your vending machine.

Another very important thing that you need to keep in mind is how to keep your machines from being vandalized and your money from getting stolen. Every vending machine owner is bound to experience vandalism at some point in their business, this could be in the form of products being stolen or your money being stolen from your machine. You can follow these steps to ensure your machines are safe from vandalism:

Build relationships: Try to avoid just going to locations to refill your machines. You would need to try and build relationships with the people in the general vicinity of your vending machines, this is because people who feel they have a connection with you are generally less likely to steal from you. Take some time to talk or joke around with the people you often see in your location and make a point of asking these individuals what their favorite items are. This will not only help you to build relationships but it will also help you to figure out what the best products are to stock and supply to your clientele. Another great way of protecting your vending machines, stock, and profits is placing your machines on the inside of buildings.

Vending machines placed outside may be more prone to thieves and troublemakers, although they may make you a good amount of profit.

Alarm System: Although alarm systems for vending machines can be quite costly, the advancement in technology is making these systems more affordable. The average alarm system can cost anywhere between $80 and $100 and can be installed at a moderate amount.

Stickers and Signs: Should you not be able to afford an alarm system for your vending machines right away, you can opt to get stickers that you can place on your vending machines telling individuals that you may deter thieves and vandals. Examples of what kind of wording you can use on these stickers are:

- Warning: Alarm System Active on this Vending Machine. Any Movement Wil Set Off The Alarm

- All Cash and Coins Removed Daily

You would want to print stickers on bright red or orange sticker paper so it can be visible to anyone looking to make trouble with your machines.

Vending Machine Cage: Although placing a cage over your vending machine may affect sales, it could help prevent vandalism and theft. You can consider this option for machines that are active during the day but receive little to no activity at night.

Security Cameras: Another effective way of protecting your vending machines is by installing a security camera to watch over your vending machine. You may need to ask permission before you can do this because they will need to be connected to an electrical system. Should the location seem extra dodgy, you might want to reconsider placing your machine there in the first place.

Business Insurance: As mentioned in previous chapters, business insurance is a must-have for any business. Business insurance can help cover you against theft and vandalism. Business insurance can help you to repair or replace any broken machines, although they don't help to prevent theft or vandalism. One thing to keep in mind with business insurance is that when you submit multiple claims for the same machine in the same location, your insurance company may refuse to pay or they may increase your premiums or cancel your policy altogether.

Vending Machine Locks and Keys: Buying new machines would mean you have the only set of keys to access your vending machine. However, when you buy a preowned machine, you may want to change the locks and keys as soon as possible. This can prevent vandalism from other companies or even the previous owner looking to sabotage your operation. Changing the locks and keys to your vending machines is quite cheap so it is the perfect preventative measure to safeguard your machines.

So the next subject we will be touching on is the profit margin you should be aiming for with your vending machine business. To reach your profit goals you need to make the best possible decisions for your business and focus on building your business for the long term instead of just focusing on the short term. Instead of running head-on and planning to make thousands of dollars to start with, you should commit your time to learning all you can to succeed in the vending business. You need to realize that you need more than one machine to make a significant amount of income; making thousands of dollars with only one or two machines is almost impossible. You need to do your market research and be willing to change your products, adjust your prices, move your machines, and get new locations regularly to increase your profit. All of these practices will positively impact your profit margins in the long run if done properly.

Another great way to ensure profitability in your vending business is to invest in proper vending machine software from the start. Vend-Trak is one such example. This software will track your machines, products, and location, and will empower you to take steps in the right direction. In the vending business, you should be aiming for at least $1 profit on every transaction. Although this may not be possible for every kind of product you sell, this should be your target. There are vending machine owners who work towards a revenue market of $300 per month, broken down this would be 10 transactions per day on average to meet their numbers.

Should you be unhappy with the location in which you placed your vending machine, and you are considering removing your vending machine, you need to think the agreement that you and the owner of the location entered into. You need to be wary of every stipulation in your agreement so you are not breaching the contract and possibly placing your business in trouble with the client. Once you and the owner have agreed on the removal of your vending machine, you will be able to remove or relocate your vending machine should you have a more popular location in mind.

Another common problem vending machine owners encounter is individuals or other business owners gaining access to their machines. It all depends on the type of machine you are looking to place at locations, but the possibility of your locks looking similar to your competitors is often very high. Keys to your vending machine may also be available on eBay, and individuals with ill intentions will purchase these keys to cash in on your hard work. Mechanical and electronic locks are available for your vending machines and are possibly the best option to keep your machines safe.

Mechanical locks: When installing a mechanical lock, you need to be aware of the internal mechanism inside the machine, as long as a lock has tension and counter tension, it can be accessed. Plug locks, padlocks, 5-pin or 7-pin numbers, and even flat key locks can all be picked when using the correct set of tools. Tubular keys are the best type to prevent locks from being picked; because tubular locks are placed in a circle, bump keying will not be effective. Should you be worried about your locks getting drilled, you might want to consider getting an anti-drill lock made of hardened steel. You would need to find out what type of lock will be the best for a certain application.

Electronic locks: Electronic locks are great to use for preventing internal and external vandalism. They only open at specific times while using a specific set of keys. These types of keys give you a log of when your machine has been opened and what key was used to open it, this makes the process of identifying issues so much easier. Electronic keys come with a low-security remote-controlled key, similar to a garage door opener. This adds an extra layer of security to the business owner. Electronic locks can be programmed yourself using your computer although this does not prevent your locks from being vandalized by the use of a drill or your machines being physically broken into. These locks can be quite expensive as well as lost keys, so you need to be sure that you keep your keys safe and your locks protected.

Quality locks: Purchasing a high-quality lock could mean you will receive a patented key design which makes it more difficult for criminals to purchase keys to your locks and this, in turn, increases the security of your machines. These locks have a hardened steel face with a steel pin on the inside.

One thing to look for when purchasing a lock for your vending machine, ensure that it meets NAMA specifications. Nama has an extremely high standard for locks and T-handles in the United States. The NAMA specifications guarantee that you will receive a quality product with confidence that the lock will fit any standard vending machine.

Let's discuss some of the common problems that vending machine owners have and how you can remedy them:

How do I notify customers when there is a price increase?

You can place a note on the inside of your vending machine against the glass so it cannot be removed or you can place a notice on the outside of the machine but make sure that it cannot easily be removed.

What can I do when my machine only dispenses cans from one slot?

Firstly check that all your motors are running and ensure that you have at least six cans in every column to satisfy the sold-out switches.

My cold temperature is too low and it is freezing the condiments.

You may want to check your relay to ensure that it is working properly and make adjustments to your temperature through programming your board under the 'refrig' menu.

My machine is making a strange noise in the compressor.

Your condenser fans are common for noises and often need to be replaced.

My machine keeps tripping the circuit breaker.

Unplug your compressor and plug in the machine to see if it still pops the circuit breaker.

What can I do when my machine cord is too short?

For refrigerated machines, do not use an extension cord. Some machines have an extra length of cord inside the machine behind the strain relief. Look for this before considering a wire stretcher.

There is a rattling noise when my refrigerator/compressor turns on.

Your compressor fan may be wearing out. The

core is moving around making the noise, you may also want to tighten the legs of the fan. Should the rattling continue when the fan is disconnected, then the compressor may have a different issue.

How do I fix the display on my food and drink machine when it isn't showing?

This could be a possible loose harness between the logic board and display board.

My tray won't spin enough to drop a product.

Place a product pusher behind your products if necessary.

My bill validator won't accept a second bill for the same purchase.

You can start by turning off escrow and force vend, then turn the machine off for a few minutes and turn it back on. Ensure that your machine is stocked with quarters, nickels, and dimes. Use only coins for the first vend, and make sure you use one of each coin. Then you can try and use two-dollar bills and see if that solves the problem.

There is frost on my evaporator. How do I remedy this?

Your machine might be low on freon caused by leaks. You can fill it up but there is no way of knowing how long this will last. If there is any additional moisture near your machine, you would need to clean it up.

What should I do when buying machines privately?
Find out why the buyer is selling, personally inspect the

machine for faults, do your due diligence and speak to previous buyers who have engaged in business from that individual.

Do I need to write up a contract?

We recommend getting a professional contract drafted by a lawyer, or online using sites such as www.RocketLawyer.com

Am I at risk of a lawsuit if a machine falls on someone?

To prevent your machines from falling over, you can get anti-tip stickers or L-brackets to mount your machines to the wall. You should also check serial numbers for any of the equipment sporting bottler logos. You must get liability insurance to ensure that you are well covered should the unexpected happen.

How can I prevent my machines from being broken into and robbed?

Thieves often push the button and hope that the lock bolt being in the t-handle base is facing down. When they push the button the t-handle pops open. You can prevent this by placing a piece of PVC pipe over the base of the t-handle to cover those holes and prevent break-ins. You should also put a hose clamp at the end of the PVC pipe to keep it in place. You may also want to place lock covers over your machine locks for additional security. Medeco offer high-quality locks that cost around $20 each with their own key. You may need to always buy from them once you set up your account.

Chapter 6:
General Business and Tax Advice

"What is the difference between a taxidermist and a tax collector? The taxidermist takes only the skin."

Mark Twain

First and foremost, let's discuss the topic of tax deductibles. A section 179 tax deduction is good for both new and used equipment, including off-the-shelf software. The equipment needs to be purchased or financed the same year in which you make the deduction for it to take effect. The maximum spending gap for equipment purchases is $2,700,000, once this amount is exceeded, the tax amount will be reduced to a dollar for dollar basis. Section 179 works in the following ways:

• Qualified equipment was often written off a little at a time through the help of depreciation, although this has changed and company owners can write off the entire amount of the equipment purchased in the same year that it was purchased. This has significantly impacted how companies can reduce their tax liabilities because they can deduct the full amount instead of waiting to deduct it over a few years.

Section 179 is possibly the best deduction you can make for your small business and I will discuss it a bit more below. The information above is general information related to a section 179 deduction and should be kept in mind throughout the rest of this section. I have provided an example of a section 179 deduction to better explain how it works

> Equipment Purchased: $1,150,000
>
> First Year Write Off: $1,080,000
>
> ($1,080,000 maximum for 2022)
>
> 100% Bonus First Year Depreciation: $100,000
>
> (updated to 100% via 'Tax Cuts and Jobs Act')
>
> Normal First Year Depreciation: $0
>
> (20% in each of 5yrs on remaining amount)
>
> Total First Year Deduction: $1,150,000
>
> ($1,050,000+100,000+0)
>
> Cash Savings: $402,500
>
> ($1,150,000x35% tax rate)
>
> Equipment cost after tax: $747,500
>
> (assuming a 35% tax bracket)

The section 179 tax deduction is not difficult to understand, this IRS tax code allows businesses to deduct the full purchase price of qualified equipment they purchased or financed during the tax year. In layman's terms, this means that any qualified equipment that you purchased or leased can be deducted in full from your gross income. This incentive has been created by the US government to encourage business owners to invest in themselves. A few years ago this deduction was referred to as the 'SUV Tax Loophole' or 'Hummer Deduction,' this is because business owners used this deduction to write off the purchase of qualified vehicles at the time. This has been significantly reduced over recent years. This means that the Section 179 deduction is more beneficial to small businesses than ever. This deduction has been included in the Stimulus act and Congressional Tax Bills, and although larger incorporations can also benefit from this deduction, it is more targeted toward providing tax relief for small businesses. There are millions of small businesses that are taking action and reaping the benefits of making use of this deduction.

How the section 179 deduction used to work in previous years, allowed business owners to deduct their equipment over a few years as the price depreciated. This means that should you have paid $50,000 on one machine, you would have been able to deduct $10,000 over five years. Although this was better than having no write-offs at all, most businesses would prefer to write off the entire amount at once for the purchased equipment. This is exactly what section 179 allows business owners to do. This has improved the ways businesses operate and the economy in general. This has also allowed businesses to purchase equipment as needed instead of having to wait until previous equipment has been completely deducted.

Any business that purchases or leases new or used equipment during the year are eligible for the section 179 deduction. For equipment to be eligible for the section 179 deduction, it has to be purchased and put into use between January 1, 2022, and December 31, 2022.

The Section 179 deduction often comes with a bonus depreciation which is offered on rotating years. For the year 2022, it is offered at 100%. In previous years the section 179 deduction only covered new equipment but the legislation has been adapted to include used equipment as well. The bonus depreciation is, however, more useful for larger businesses who often spend more than the $2,700,000 cap on new capital equipment, and they can deduct some of the cost of the new equipment as well as carry forward the loss. One requirement that the Section 179 deduction does have is that any equipment deduction from this should be used at least 50% of the time for business purposes to qualify.

I will provide a list of qualifying properties that you can deduct using the Section 179 deduction:

- Equipment purchased for business use
- Tangible property for business use
- Business vehicles exceeding 6,000 lbs
- Computers
- Off-the-shelf computer software
- Office furniture
- Office equipment
- Property attached to your building like printing press, large manufacturing tools, and equipment.
- Partial property use, property used for both personal and business use.

- Improvements were made to non-residential buildings like fire suppression, alarms, security systems, HVAC, and roof repairs.

Keep in mind that the above qualify whether the products are purchased, leased, or financed, both new and used. Section 179 helps small businesses to have more purchasing power, and with recent changes, small businesses have new deduction limits.

Now let's take a deeper look into the tax obligations you will have as a self-employed business owner. Self-employed individuals typically have to pay self-employment (SE) tax and income tax. Social Security and Medicare taxes fall primarily under self-employment tax and are aimed at individuals who work for themselves. This is similar to the taxes withheld from the salary earned by regular employees. This is primarily referred to as Social Security and Medicare taxes and not any other income taxes. When you determine if you are eligible for self-employment tax and income tax, you need to determine the net profit or loss you are experiencing from your business. You can do this by subtracting your expenses from your income. Should your income be more than your expenses, then the difference would be classified as net profit. This will then be inserted onto page 1 of Form 1040 or 1040-SR. When your expenses exceed your income, this will be classified as a net loss. You need to file an income tax return when your net earnings are more than $400.

You only need to file when your earnings are less than $400 if you meet the other filling requirements listed in Form 1040 or 1040-SR instructions. Form 1040-ES,

Estimated Tax for Individuals, is used to estimate these taxes. You would need your annual tax return from the previous year to complete Form 1040-ES. You can use the Electronic Federal Tax Payment System (EFTPS) to mail your estimated tax payments, or you may make payments using this system. During your first year of operation, you may need to estimate the amount you expect to make for the year. Should your estimation be too high, you might need to complete another Form 1040-ES worksheet to refigure your estimated tax for the next quarter. Should your estimation be too low, then you would once again complete another Form 1040-ES to recalculate your estimated taxes for the next quarter.

You would need to complete a Schedule C to report the income or loss you experience from your business as a sole proprietor. You can also use Schedule C's income or loss calculator to calculate the taxes you were obligated to pay during the tax year. The business structure you choose plays an important role when it's time to file your taxes. Limited Liability Companies are often the best business structure to use.

The following question you may be asking, is how often you should be paying taxes for your own business? The answer to this question would be quarterly. When paying your taxes once a year you could incur penalties on your taxes, and this could lead to a hefty amount that needs to be paid. Quarterly tax payments should be filed on the 15th of January, April, June, and September. Should the 15th fall on a Friday then the deadline will be moved to the following Monday. You can estimate how much you would need to pay by using Form 1040-ES, which offers a variety of venues to assist entrepreneurs in estimating their tax payments. Your tax payments can be made via phone, mail, direct pay, or debit/credit options.

To beat your competitors in the vending machine industry, it is important to know the best strategies, which we will discuss now.

- **Location:** When dealing with vending machines, you need to make sure that the location where you place your machines will be profitable and assist with the growth of your business. You would need to make sure that there is enough foot traffic for these individuals to make use of your vending machines. Placing your vending machines in places like malls, schools, or establishments with many offices is often the best option when you are trying to grow your business quickly.

- **Product:** Once your vending machine is placed, you should determine which products you would want to supply to your customers. To do this, you would need to find out what your clients want to purchase and go from there.

- **Different locations:** Having vending machines in different locations could be quite profitable for your business. The amount of profit you will be willing to generate with several machines could give your business a significant boost. You should always be on the lookout for new locations to increase your profit, instead of just working with the locations you currently have.

- **Working machines:** You should always ensure that all your machines are in perfect working condition to ensure that your customers will be able to purchase their favorite products from your machines. Making a point of regularly checking your machines is of utmost importance, especially when it will affect your bottom line.

When starting your own business, you would need to ensure that every opportunity to make extra money is leveraged to its fullest potential to make your company better. You should also be aware of any possible developments that your company may need to improve.

Knowing your strengths when starting your vending machine business is very important. Whether that is research, sales, or your ability to communicate, you would need to use your strengths to build your vending machine business. There is no specified strength that I can give you to focus on because it will all depend on your knowledge and experience, and you would need to harness that to make a success of your business. Take a minute to figure out what sets you apart from your competition and what you can harness to increase your leverage over your competition.

The tax rate you will be paying depends highly on the state in which you are operating your business. I have done some research on the different sales tax rates per state so you can have a better idea of what you will be paying according to your operating region. Most states have a set tax ranging between 4% and 7%. The average rate is around 5.09%, some states are above, and some are below this rate. California is possibly the only state with a sales tax rate of over 7% and also has the largest population. Colorado has a sales tax of 2.9% and states like Oregon, New Hampshire, Montana, Delaware, and Alaska have a

0% sales tax rate. The ten states with the highest sales tax rates are:

- California (7.25%)
- Indiana (7.0%)
- Mississippi (7.00%)
- Rhode Island (7.00%)
- Tennessee (7.00%)
- Minnesota (6.88%)
- Nevada (6.85%)
- New Jersey (6.63%)
- Arkansas(6.50%)
- Kansas (6.50%)

The following table will display the sales tax rates per state for 2022.

State

State Tax Rate

Average Local Tax

Combined Rate

2022 Population

California

7.25%

1.31%

8.56%

39,664,128

Tennessee

7.00%

2.47%

9.47%

7,001,803

Rhode Island

7.00%

0.00%

7.00%

1,062,583

Mississippi

7.00%

0.07%

7.07%

2,961,536

Indiana

7.00%

0.00%

7.00%

6,842,385

Minnesota

6.88%

0.55%

7.43%

5,739,781

Nevada

6.85%

1.29%

8.14%

3,238,601

New Jersey

6.63%

-0.03%

6.60%

8,870,685

Washington

6.50%

2.67%

9.17%

7,887,965

Kansas

6.50%

2.17%

8.67%

2,919,179

Arkansas

6.50%

2.93%

9.43%

3,042,017

Connecticut

6.35%

0.00%

6.35%

3,546,588

Texas

6.25%

1.94%

8.19%

30,097,526

Massachusetts

6.25%

0.00%

6.25%

6,922,107

Illinois

6.25%

2.49%

8.74%

12,518,071

West Virginia

6.00%

0.39%

6.39%

1,755,715

Vermont

6.00%

0.18%

6.18%

622,882

South Carolina

6.00%

1.43%

7.43%

5,342,388

Pennsylvania

6.00%

0.34%

6.43%

12,805,190

Michigan

6.00%

0.00%

6.00%

9,995,212

Maryland

6.00%

0.00%

6.00%

6,075,314

Kentucky

6.00%

0.00%

6.00%

4,487,233

Iowa

6.00%

0.82%

6.82%

3,174,426

Idaho

6.00%

0.03%

6.03%

1,896,652

Florida

6.00%

1.05%

7.05%

22,177,997

Utah

5.95%

0.99%

6.94%

3,363,182

Ohio

5.75%

1.42%

7.17%

11,727,377

Arizona

5.60%

2.77%

8.37%

7,640,796

Nebraska

5.50%

1.35%

6.85%

1,960,790

Maine

5.50%

0.00%

5.50%

1,359,677

Virginia

5.30%

0.35%

5.65%

8,638,218

New Mexico

5.13%

2.69%

7.82%

2,109,093

Wisconsin

5.00%

0.44%

5.44%

5,867,518

North Dakota

5.00%

1.85%

6.85%

774,008

North Carolina

4.75%

2.22%

6.97%

10,807,491

South Dakota

4.50%

1.90%

6.40%

902,542

Oklahoma

4.50%

4.42%

8.92%

4,007,179

Louisiana

4.45%

5.00%

9.45%

4,616,106

Missouri

4.23%

3.90%

8.13%

6,184,843

Wyoming

4.00%

1.36%

5.36%

582,233

New York

4.00%

4.49%

5.36%

19,223,191

Hawaii

4.00%

0.41%

8.49%

1,401,709

Georgia

4.00%

3.29%

4.41%

10,936,299

Alabama

4.00%

5.14%

7.29%

4,949,697

Colorado

2.90%

4.73%

7.63%

5,961,083

Oregon

0.00%

0.00%

0.00%

4,325,290

New Hampshire

0.00%

0.00%

0.00%

1,378,449

Montana

0.00%

0.00%

0.00%

1,093,117

Delaware

0.00%

0.00%

0.00%

998,619

Alaska

0.00%

1.43%

1.43%

720,763

From my experience, here is a list of the best tax tips you can apply to your business to save you time and money:

• **Understand start-up costs:** "These costs cannot be deducted until the first sale. Then they are deducted over 15 years, and you can elect to deduct the first $5,000 in the first year of business. Many small businesses assume they can deduct all their costs in starting a new business, but they cannot until they have their first sale. Then costs are deductible based on the laws for that deduction." - Rosen.

- **Keep your records accurate:** Always make sure that your accounting records are as accurate as possible, this will make your tax filing journey more convenient.

- **Understand financial jargon:** Starting a business is a challenge in itself, and when the financial jargon comes in you might get very confused. There are various terminologies linked to accounting and it would benefit you immensely if you can understand them. Take some time off and familiarize yourself with some of the most used financial jargon that you might come across. Some of the most used financial terms are:

    o **Revenue:** This is the amount of income you earn from your business in the form of product sales and services provided.

    o **COGS:** An abbreviation for the cost of goods sold, this is the amount you use to produce products that your company sells.

    o **Gross profit:** Your gross profit is the amount you receive after deducting your COGS.

    o **Net sales:** The total income after you have deducted all your business expenses.

- **Keep business and private finances separate:** Opening a separate account dedicated to business income is the best option you have when starting a business. You might get into trouble with the IRS should you mix the two. The IRS will not find issues with your set of records should they be kept separate. Doing this will also simplify your process of filing your taxes.

- **Using accounting software:** Although using an excel spreadsheet is a cost-effective way of managing your business finances, it also poses a greater amount of risk. Human error is often unavoidable and this could cost your business greatly. Excel can also not be used to draft financial statements for you and it will not be able to tell you about your largest vendors and what you bought from them during the year. Obtaining specialized accounting software (i.e. Xero, Quickbooks) is our best option to save time, reduce errors and provide you with automated reports. You can understand your business finance, increase cash flow, and calculate deductions with an accounting program.

- **Tracking your inventory:** An important part of your business operations is keeping track of your inventory value. This is the amount of money you have designated for unsold inventory. The cost of the products you sell will often change from year to year, and you need to keep track of these costs accurately. You would need to track this at least once a month.

- **Understanding tax deductibles:** The simple truth is that the lower profitability your company has, the less tax you would need to pay. Two types of business expenses are tax-deductible according to the IRS:

    o **Ordinary business expenses:** These are the same expenses used by various companies in the same industry.

- **Necessary business expenses:** These expenses are used to help you grow your business and are considered to be necessary.

• This does not, however, mean that you can deduct just any expense. Below are the most common business expenses that are tax-deductible:

- Marketing
- Shipping/Delivery
- Utilities
- Insurance
- Equipment
- Commercial leases
- Accounting/legal services
- Payroll

• **Paying quarterly taxes:** Businesses who predict that their taxes will be $1,000 or more for the year are recommended to make quarterly payments. You can pay quarterly taxes on the following dates:

- April 15
- June 15
- September 15
- January 15

• **Donating to charity:** Donating to charity will significantly reduce your tax liability. There are however limitations to donating to charity, including:

o An individual can donate and write off up to 100% of their taxable income.

o Corporations can donate/write off up to 25% of their taxable income.

o Donating to charity can not only help you reduce your taxes, but it can also help you to connect with your market and individuals will be more likely to use your services because they will associate you with someone who has strong community values.

- **Keep money aside for payroll taxes:** The moment you start employing individuals you would need to withhold, report and pay payroll taxes. The three main taxes you need to take note of are Social Security taxes, Medicare taxes, and federal income taxes.

- **Contributing to your retirement account:** Retirement account contributions are tax-deductible. When contributing some of your business profits to your, or your employee's 401(k) plans, you can save significantly on your tax returns.

- **Section 179:** A section 179 form from the IRS can help you to deduct the cost of certain items as expenses. When certain items are used for business purposes then you can ultimately write them off from your tax return and reduce your liability.

- **Business income deduction:** When your business has less than $170,050 you can qualify for this deduction. Your income level, wages, assets, and the type of assets you have play a big role in the factors to determine your eligibility.

- **Bonus depreciation:** This deduction allows you to deduct the purchase price of business-related equipment from your business income. You can deduct a yearly amount associated with this equipment. The most important advantage of this deduction is there is no limit to it. It can create a net loss for your business and take away from future taxable income.

- **Preparing for tax season:** You won't want to prepare for your tax returns at the last possible moment, for this reason, you would need to adequately prepare for your tax return in advance. The best time to start planning for your tax return is during November of the previous year. This will help you to create a realistic forecast of your company's tax situation and you will have enough time to plan.

- **Home office deduction:** Deducting your home office can be quite valuable but keep in mind that the space you are deducting needs to be used strictly for business purposes. This deduction is also not valid should you be renting an office away from your home. To calculate your home office deduction, you need to measure the square footage of your office and multiply it by $5.

- **Standard vs actual automobile deductions:** Having a look at both methods will help you determine which will give you the best benefits. Keep in mind that before switching, you might face some restrictions. The two methods are:

    ○ **Standard method:** You get $0,58 per mile, including tolls and parking.

- **Actual method:** This includes all automobile expenses multiplied by the business percentage (total miles for the year).

- **Note:** Should your office be located in your home, you can start adding up for this deduction from the minute you step outside of your home.

• **Postpone income and pay in advance:** To save even more on your business tax you can delay sending out invoices on products or services rendered. Another way is paying in advance for things like your rent, or purchasing office equipment. You can charge these expenses to your credit card as these are also deductible for tax purposes.

• **Pay family members:** "You can hire your kids to work on your business. As a result, you are effectively shifting your business income to a lower tax bracket. However, make sure that you are keeping records regarding the time spent, nature of the job, and the legitimate pay rate," Dalmacio.

• **Organize the small things:** All those little purchases and sales can become quite a task to keep track of. For this reason, you would need to have a system in place to keep track of them that works for you. Even these small amounts can add up to big ones when left out.

• **Loss deductions:** Whether you are an S corporation, partnership, LLC, or sole proprietorship, losses incurred can be deducted from your income tax return immediately.

• **Professional fees:** When you are using the services of tax professionals, lawyers, and other consultants on a once-off or ongoing basis, you can write off their fees against your tax return.

The following are some of the best tips and tricks I've learned to create a profitable business, and these tips are especially important when you are just starting out:

• **Be fearless:** One of the biggest hurdles you will face when starting your own business is the fear of jumping in the first place. Many individuals are scared of what would happen if they leave their paid job to start their ventures. You would need to learn to control your fears when it comes to starting your own business. The true test of controlling your fears comes when you need to make conversations at conferences, make sales on major deals, cut ties with partners, and watch a business fail. Remember that the person who can fail but is not scared to get back up, dust themselves off and try again are truly fearless.

• **Understand finance:** The truth regarding finance when starting a business is not that you need to be rich to get started, but you would still need some money to invest. The important thing to remember is not how much money you have but rather how your finances work and how you can use the funds available to you in the smartest way possible. The reality behind people who live paycheck to paycheck is that they often fill their lives with liabilities like car and house payments, credit cards, and materialistic things that ultimately take their money. Financially literate individuals know to understand that they can use the money available to them to build assets or things that make them more money. To be successful, you would need to know how to use money and make it work for you.

- **Use your leverage:** It takes a certain mindset to think outside the box and find new relationships and circumstances. You would need to know what to do when new opportunities present themselves to you. Individuals who are often too scared to leave their day jobs to follow their dream also can't leverage the assets and relationships in their lives. Finding new ways to create profits and opportunities every day is part of being a successful entrepreneur. Take the quote, "When life hands you lemons, make lemonade" some people will make lemonade and drink it themselves, while a successful businessman will sell the lemonade to buy more lemons and invest in another business model.

- **Having the right attitude:** Success in business matters only when it equates to the success you have in life, and this all comes from having the right attitude. It's necessary to know what is important to you in life and to build your success around that. It's truly a great thing when you want to start a business to gain financial freedom, but the true question is, what will you do with those riches once you have them in your grasp? Changing your mindset to using your funds to help others and solve problems is the right one to have, and you will ultimately achieve true happiness because you will be improving the lives of those around you.

- **Showing gratitude:** You should be happy in both your business and personal lives because this would mean that you are grateful for the world you are living in. Remember to never forget the people, places, and things that have played a role in your lives that helped you reach success.

- **Stay healthy:** What is the purpose of making a ton of money if you won't be able to use it due to reckless behavior? You would need to think about the impact certain things have on your life and your future. After all, you wouldn't want to work, and by the time your business reaches its peak you are no longer here. As entrepreneurs, we are often so focused on the tasks at hand that we forget about the other things that are just as important like taking a breath or eating a healthy meal at lunchtime. Too many times individuals who are so hell-bent on making a success of their business, spend their nights consumed in alcohol and drugs just to get rid of the stress they may have faced during the day. Remember that without your health you can never truly reach success, and by saying this I am not just referring to our physical health but our mental health as well. You need to be able to enjoy the road you are taking and not allow it to turn you into a ball of stress.

- **Listen to your customer:** One of the most important steps to being successful in business is being able to listen to your customers and provide services they will appreciate. The best way of ensuring customer satisfaction is to know what the pain points in your business are and which customers are experiencing these pain points. Understanding your target audience will help you not only with the products and services you are offering but also how to advertise to reach potential customers and help you save money on uninterested audiences.

- **When to be transparent:** Transparency can be as dangerous as it is beneficial, but you should know when to disclose information and when you should keep quiet.

This takes time and experience to learn, but it is important to keep in mind.

- **Trust your gut:** Your instincts are your best tool in business and it's very valuable to your decision-making process. You would need to know when to follow your instincts and when to follow advice from others.

- **Learn from others in the industry:** Newcomers in certain industries are often given very warm welcomes. When you open yourself to people who have been in the game for a while, they will be more than willing to share their experiences with you and give you some insider tips.

- **Ask for help:** When starting your business, don't be afraid to ask for help should you get stuck in a certain area of your business. Reach out to other business owners or mentors for insight on how to move forward. Don't feel alone in the journey of starting your business; there are a lot of people out there who are ready and willing to help.

- **Reduce uncertainty and increase certainty:** You should reduce as much uncertainty in your business as possible when starting. Having a lot of questions is normal when starting a business. If you were able to get all the answers to your questions instantly, then there wouldn't be an opportunity. Validate your assumptions early to reduce uncertainty.

- **Leverage your comparative advantage:** Have a look at your nearest competitors and find out what gives you an advantage over them, and then use it to build up your business. Whatever your skills or knowledge, use that to your advantage and grow your business to amazing heights.

Now that I have provided you with the tips to make your business a success, I would like for you to know why most businesses fail and what you should avoid if you want to become a successful business owner:

- **No marketing:** A marketing strategy is a perfect way to see whether a company will succeed. Marketing can help you find customers as well as sell them new products and services that you are offering, but without one, you are likely to not gain new customers, and this could be detrimental to your business.

- **Poor customer service:** Another thing that you would need to provide your customers with is excellent customer service, this will help them to trust you and to build a professional relationship with you. Customers are not interested in working with people they have to struggle to get a hold of to perform certain tasks. You would need to do everything in your power at all times to keep your customers content with your business.

- **No plan for scaling:** You need to be prepared for what your business can bring to you. Should you start a business as a side hustle and it grows to such heights that you would need to put in more hours, then you would need to be prepared for that. The last thing you would want to do is close your business because you weren't ready for the enormous growth in a short period and you are left short-handed or short on time.

- **No need:** Another major reason businesses close down is because individuals create products that might seem great at the time, but the sad fact is there is absolutely no demand for them. Doing market research and applying due diligence is the only way to ensure that you will be providing the best for your clients. You would need to get in touch with your target audience and find out if they will be willing to purchase your items from you and if they are willing to pay the price you have put on your items. Another big problem is the lack of funds you would need capital, investments, loans, or revenue to get through those difficult times, this is where a detailed budget comes into play to help you work better with your available finances.

- **Too much competition:** A saturated market is never something you would want to enter into, it can mean that your business will be at a disadvantage right from the start. Even though it is not impossible to enter the market should your products, prices, and customer relations be better than your competitors, you still need to do your research to understand exactly what is expected from you to beat your competitors.

A final word of advice I can give on starting your own business and to close off my tips and tricks is to do your research and actively work towards reaching your goals. Success does not happen overnight and it takes a lot of time and effort. And the best advice I can give is there is no better time to start than right now!

Chapter 7:
Insider Secrets From My Experience & Deal Analysis

"Motivation is what gets you started, habit is what keeps you going."

Jim Rohn

The first story I found from a successful vending machine business owner was from Steve and his father. They met a vending machine distributor who had promised them two machines with locations that would give them a significant return on their investment. Without hesitation, they paid $5,000 on a promise that the salesman made with the hope of making a living off their vending machines. Although Steve and his father didn't lose out completely on this promise, they did notice that the locations they received weren't performing as well as they had hoped for. They then asked the distributor to provide them with better locations, but he refused. Now, although their story might not have had a happy ending, I have compiled a few insider secrets about the vending machine business; and one of the first ones is to get a written agreement. This agreement needs to stipulate what type of locations you will be getting for the investment you are making.

It may be a bit unreasonable to expect a distributor to give you a sure answer about the profitability of a vending machine or location, but there are other things that you can negotiate. You may want to negotiate the amount of traffic that a certain location has. Your agreement would need to stipulate that your vending machine be placed in a building with upwards of 100 individuals on-site every day. This will ensure that your business will be profitable, and you will receive a steady stream of income from the machines that are on site. Not making this requirement clear could mean that you will end up with a location only receiving a few sets of feet moving through every day and this could lead to a greater loss than gain in the long run. You may also want to include a non-compete clause, this will ensure that you won't be competing with existing vending machines in the location. A pre-approval clause is also something to consider, this will allow you to have a look at the machines before they get delivered. You need to look out for the potential landmines within the vending machine business, you should also learn how to step over them so you can create a profitable business.

There is no doubt that the vending machine business is:

Simple: When machines are located close to each other, all of them can be serviced in one day. All you would need to do is stock them and collect the funds.

Lucrative: With between 10 and 20 machines, you can make upwards of $10,000 a month.

Flexible: This business is designed for almost everyone, whether you want to do it part-time or become a bigger player, you can do that with a vending machine business. Some of the biggest players in the vending industry have between 500 and 1,000 vending machines in different locations.

The steps you need to take to start your vending machine business have been explained throughout the book, but I would like to address another successful tool you would need to have to make it successful. That is, the power of persuasion. Before I get into the underbelly of the power of persuasion, it's important to keep in mind that not everyone will be as easily persuaded and some may take a bit more to make up their minds. Let's take an example of looking for a new car, you might already have the make, model, cost, and color in mind. But despite all these considerations, you are careful of being pushed into buying it. Should the salesman that is helping you be overly pushy or aggressive, you might decide against buying a car and leave without purchasing it. The reason for this example is so you know that people are wary of being manipulated. When trying to persuade someone to do something, you should do everything to not scare them off, and that is possibly the most effective persuasion technique to remember, don't be too aggressive.

One way of persuasion you can use is a technique called visualization. Marketers using the art of visualization allow you to think about the bigger picture. The art of visualization is showing your client on paper what they will gain through using your product or service, and in a way making them believe that they need it.

The first step you would need to do is to get to know your prospective client. Finding out exactly what your client needs is an important part of the way you are trying to persuade them. You will have a clearer image of what you will need to present to your client and your visualization tool will be more effective.

Painting a realistic picture is your next step to success. Should the person you are trying to persuade still think they can live without the service you are offering, then your visualization tactic may not work. You need to know what image to present to your prospect to trigger an emotional response and what will get them to accept the image as a potential reality. By doing this, you will have no trouble persuading them to buy your service or product. Having the visualization tool in your arsenal will help you immensely when obtaining clients for your business.

The best way to avoid failure is by learning from individuals who have tried and failed and decided to share their experiences with you to learn from and improve on them.

Incorrectly Calculating Payback: Projecting your expected profits from your vending machine business is possibly one of the most common mistakes new business owners make. Companies who supply vending machines often tell their customers that they will be able to make back the cost of their machines within six months, but in reality, it can take between 12 and 14 months for your machines to pay themselves off. There are many newcomers to the industry who take on more than they can handle on the promise of a machine paying itself off within six months, and this can ultimately harm their business. Learning how to accurately estimate the profits you can make from your business is the first step to creating a successful one from the start.

Older and Simpler Machines: To save on costs, many new business owners opt for older or simpler vending machines to service their locations. Although this might be a good idea to start with, it could mean profit loss in the long term. For you to compete with other companies, your machines need to be reliable and safe as well as have the most recent technological advances so they can serve a wider range of customers.

Faulty Pay Systems and Bill Validators: Having machines that don't dispense a product or doesn't take customers' money could lead to a significant loss in profit. Customers might not want to buy from your machines anymore, and this will ultimately harm your business even after you have resolved the problems. This is why you need to ensure your machines are working 100% before placing them in locations.

Leasing Vending Machines: Taking credit when purchasing machines or leasing machines from another company can take away from your profits, leaving you with less to work with within your company. Starting a vending machine business is great, but you would need to be sure of the costs you are incurring so your business can grow. Furthermore, leverage is adding additional risk into your business.

Purchasing Machines in Bulk: Buying a few machines at once is often a great idea especially when you can pay a discounted rate when purchasing more than one machine. But the reality behind this logic is that you would need to be sure of where you will be placing the machines and if they will generate an income from the start before purchasing them. Purchasing machines before having set locations could mean that you would need to store your unused machines until you find a location for them.

Wrong Places: I have mentioned this previously, but the location is key when starting a vending machine business. Having vending machines is a great start, but placing them in the wrong location can be very bad for your business. Bad locations don't have a lot of foot traffic or they have machines from other companies who are taking the attention away from your machines. Placing your machines near cafes, diners or restaurants can also significantly lower your profit margins because these places will be preferred above your vending machines.

Buying Habits of Your Customers: You should know your customer and your location. Placing a vending machine in a lower-income area and then still expecting to ask more for your products could lead to your vending machine being unused. When securing a location ensure that you do your homework on your potential customers so you know what is expected from you and how you can optimize the location.

Poor Quality Products: When stocking your vending machines, it may make sense at the time to go for generic versions of popular snacks, but individuals buying from your machines may think differently. When it comes to vending machines people want the tried and true original products that they love. Your products are ultimately what brings your income, and substituting products to cut costs is never a good option.

Not Maintaining, Cleaning, or Servicing Your Machines: When you fail to maintain, clean, or service your vending machines on a set schedule, they may break down and leave your customers without their favorite snacks. This can affect their trust in your company and ultimately lead them to never buy products from your vending machines again. Having a set schedule of when your machines need to be maintained is a good way of ensuring that they are always in working condition.

A little more about me and how I started my vending business and grew it to where it is today. I am a vending machine business owner who has started and grown my vending machine business significantly over the past few years. I took a major risk on myself when I started this business, but have since motivated many other individuals to do what I have been doing. I have always wanted to become an entrepreneur from the age of 16 and started my entrepreneurial journey by helping out a friend who was selling candy at school. I partnered with this friend and started selling candy with him, he gave me the funds and I had the personality to make the sales. I even used this business to raise money to go on a trip which is where everything took off for me. Initially, I wanted to get into real estate, but one of my close friends talked me into buying and placing a few vending machines, which I thought would be a great side hustle to get my real estate business up and running. I started my vending machine business to support my family and be able to do more for them.

I have a very close relationship with a vending warehouse that buys bigger vending routes and then sells smaller routes to small business owners, and this is how I got my first vending route. This route had 15 machines that started this venture. My friend split the cost of purchasing this vending route giving me eight machines, and my friend got seven. Before purchasing this route, I started with only two machines which brought in a mere $60 a month. I had to build up credibility within the first 3-4 months to build trust and start making a profit. To make these locations successful, I had a look at which products did well and which products didn't sell. I also started putting scratch-alls at the back of my products, this gave way for a buzz to happen, which drew more and more people to my vending machines in the hopes of winning. My website is a great benefit to my business as many business owners contact me through there should they want vending machines placed in their buildings. The three main ways I started generating business were cold calling, using a vending locator, and utilizing your website. I have only bought two vending routes since starting these machines; after buying my first vending route which had eight machines for $3,500, I sold four of the machines for $2,500. So at the end of the day, I only paid $1,000 for four machines, and the rest was profit. I continued working towards making my business better and increasing my profit margin. I am regularly checking on my sales and which products are selling, and which ones can be changed out for something else. One thing I learned from the vending machine businesses is that if you play it safe, you will stay poor, and I knew when I invested in this business, I could grow my business and make an extra income. One thing I cannot stress enough is making your website look as professional as possible, this will carry your business significantly. The better your website is the more business you will be able to generate from it. I also learned that I needed to be actively involved in this business, the more exposure you create for yourself the better your business will be doing in the future.

I then went on to create a 5-year plan for his business. I was aiming to make $100,000 gross sales per month just through my vending machines. As with any business getting the locations to meet these goals took some time, and I lost some of my revenue along the way but it all paid off in the end. I have found attending the National Automatic Merchandising Association (NAMA) expos to be quite informative, and you are bound to learn a lot from them. To reach financial freedom, I had to teach myself everything there is to know about the vending machine business, and I hope to share that knowledge and experience with you. Vending has been and still is a very lucrative business, and with the right guidance, I am sure you can make this business successful.

Purchasing established vending routes can give your business a significant boost, this is because these machines already have a reputation, and they are already earning an income. Now you may be asking how you can get your hands on these vending routes. The first place you would want to look is online. Websites like Dealstream.com and bizbuysell.com have a variety of vending businesses and routes for you to choose from. When considering a vending route, you can use bizbuysell to check the company's gross revenue, inventory, as well as their cash flow. Another way is to contact business brokers in your area and enquire about available vending routes that may be for sale. Before buying a vending route, I suggest you ask the current owner why they are selling, and ensure that the reason the seller gives you is viable so you don't end up with a struggling route. After talking to the seller you would need to go and inspect all the machines that are currently placed on their route. Depending on the appearance of the machine, you will be able to determine whether the route is a good buy or if you should look for something else. While you are inspecting the machines at each location, make a point of speaking to the owner or site manager of the location. They will be able to give you more insight on the location and if they think there are any potential improvements you can make that will not ultimately cost you more. Another thing to be careful of is if the current vending owner has had a rough relationship with the owner of the location. Because of this, it might be a bit more difficult for you to build a relationship with them due to the trust already being broken. You may also want to have a look at the Better Business Bureau to see if any complaints have been made against the vending machine owner.

Once you have completed your overview of the business practices and the physical assets, it's time to get to the paperwork. You may need to sign a confidentiality agreement to gain access to the financials of the company, but this is important for you to be aware of before making any kind of commitment. Your confidentiality agreement would need to be reviewed by your lawyer, so you are not signing for something that you are unaware of. With the help of an accountant, you can then start to go through at least five years of financial statements to ensure that the company is indeed making a profit with the vending machines. Another thing to keep in mind when going through the company's books is the contracts that the current business owner has in place and if they will have an advantage in the future. It's important to review these as the business owner might be wanting to sell because some of his contracts are about to expire, and he may not be sure if he will be able to renew them. Should this happen you would need to remove all the machines and spend time looking for new locations, which may cost you more time and money to achieve. Legal obligations should also be considered before you buy a vending route. Because you are buying the business, you are also buying into any legal affairs they may still have against the business. You can see if a business has any lawsuits against them by checking court records, this may be a bit tedious but will aid you in the long term. The final step you would need to take is asking for a clearance letter from the IRS so you won't be liable for unpaid taxes, as well as estimating the value of the route. The last thing you would want to do is pay more than a route is worth. A lawyer and accountant will help you to get an estimated price of a route that you can then compare with the price the seller is looking for.

Now let's discuss the final step in the process, which will be closing the deal. I would personally suggest that you pay cash for your vending route if possible, but should you not be able to do that, then you might want to consider visiting banks to obtain financing. Banks will look into your credit score before offering you a loan. You can also opt for seller financing, where the seller will give you a loan of between 30-60% of the purchase price, and you will need to cover the rest. You need to identify how much you can pay for a vending route. You can do this by having a look at the cash flow because this money will be used to pay back any loans you would need to acquire as well as living expenses.

You can place a bid on the route you are looking to purchase that is between 10 and 15% below your budget. Be cautious of not getting over-excited about buying a vending route and then spending more than your budget will allow. Your final step will be to execute the purchase agreement of your vending route, your lawyer will be able to help you draft this agreement which then needs to be signed by both you and the seller. Your purchase agreement will contain all the important information related to the purchase of the vending route, including the purchase price, and a list of inventory that is included in the purchase price. A purchase agreement should also include the seller's representations and warranties that will ultimately protect you after purchasing the vending route. Warranties should be given by the seller stating that the information provided to the buyer is correct and in line with the physical practices of the business.

Once you have purchased your vending route and all the paperwork has been finalized, you will want to consider upgrading some of the existing machines to be more user-friendly. Some of these machines may not be able to accept new forms of payments including credit cards or mobile payments, which could lead you to lose sales. Keep in mind that when you are installing credit card readers in your vending machines, you will be responsible for the monthly and transaction fees that are associated with using card readers. There is a lot of information that gets passed through and managed when a customer uses their credit card or mobile device to purchase products from vending machines and all of this information management costs money. With regards to this, you would need to be sure whether installing a credit card reader in certain locations is worth it or not. So once you have determined which of your sites will need card readers, you can take a look at the following three options about the best card readers currently on the market.

Nayax: Nayax has been around since 2005 and has become the industry standard in cashless, telemetry, management, and solutions for unattended machines. They currently have over 200,000 devices installed in machines around the world. Their card readers have both Wi-Fi and cellular network data capabilities, and they accept chip cards, swipe cards, loyalty, ApplePay, Google Wallet, PayPal, and Mobile App payments. Nayax devices are easy to install and they conform to all automated machine standards. Their terminal fee, interchange fee, acquire processing fee, and merchant account fees are included in their monthly service package. They have a $30 activation fee and a $7.95 monthly per modem maintenance fee, and they also charge 5.95% on every transaction from their card readers. (These may change - so please ensure that you contact the company directly to enquire). Nayax also offers their customers access to their mobile app, which gives them access to communicating with their customers as well as providing them with loyalty cards and vouchers that they can use through the app.

AirVend/365 Retail: AirVend was established in 2012, and in 2015 they acquired 365 retail markets; they are a privately held company operating in computers, electronic products, and components manufacturing. Unlike Nayax they only have cellular network data capabilities, although they can still accept swipe cards, Loyalty, ApplePay, Google Wallet, and mobile app payments. The AirVend device is touchless and provides nutritional info, offers cashless payment options, and sends data and alerts wirelessly as they happen. The monthly service fee associated with an AirVend device is $14.95, and their transaction fees are determined by the average purchase amount. (These may change so please ensure that you contact the company directly to enquire). The app provided by AirVend is 365Pay, they offer cashless payment and the ability to reload your account with funds to make payments.

Cantaloupe ePort: Cantaloupe ePort - formally known as USA Technologies is possibly the most established company around, they were established in 1992, and they provide wireless, cashless, micro-transactions, and networking services. Similar to AirVend, they only have cellular network data capabilities and can accept payments through swipe cards, loyalty, ApplePay, Google Wallet, and mobile app payments. Their device consists of two individual pieces, the card reader and the telemetry system, which accepts magnetic stripe cards as well as NFC technology from contactless cards and mobile wallets. They charge their customer a monthly service fee of $7.95 per month per device as well as a transaction fee of 5.95%. (These may change - so please ensure that you contact the company directly to enquire). USA Tech gives consumers access to a mobile app they named More, where they can gain access to ads and special offers, and use the app to make payments. Consumers will also be able to get rewards that they can exchange for credits or free vends.

Something that very few vending machine business owners know about is that they can place vending machines that offer more than just drinks and snacks. Like Ashleigh Stevenson, a 27-year-old from Newcastle who placed two eyelash vending machines close to her shop to supply the high demand for the product. These vending machines also provide her with an income even when her store is closed because girls who are out on the town can still access the eyelashes and complete their looks. Ashleigh has noted that her eyelash vending machines have been booming, and clients can't seem to get enough of them. She is aiming to expand and get more machines placed soon to service more locations and make herself more visible to a growing client base. She is selling her eyelashes for $10.99, and this makes it even more popular with clients.

Above and beyond an eyelash vending machine, you may also want to consider placing vending machines offering the following products:

- **Baby products:** Wipes, diapers, and packed food can be very lucrative in a vending machine. These vending machines can be placed near shopping arcades, supermarkets, playschools, nurseries, and daycare centers.

- **Stationary:** Pens, notebooks, erasers, and pencils can sell well from a vending machine. These vending machines will be highly lucrative outside schools, colleges, and other establishments that have individuals who need stationery daily.

- **Mobile accessories:** Mobile accessories are one of the things that we often forget when traveling. This can make this type of vending machine in places like offices, colleges, airports, or train stations quite attractive. You can add chargers, power banks, headphones, Bluetooth devices, and mobile covers to these vending machines.

These are just some of the most lucrative ideas I have found; there are many more to choose from. Vending does not just have to include snacks and beverages, rather the world is your oyster, and you can sell whatever your heart desires should there be a demand for it.

Amidst the Coronavirus pandemic, more and more locations are making vending machines available that dispense hand sanitizer, disposable masks, gloves, and anti-bacterial wipes. The first location that has made this available is the McCarran International Airport in Las Vegas.

"It's not unthinkable that someone will show up at the airport and has left behind one of these items that's almost essential now to air travel."

Christine Crews

These machines can help the public to practice good hygiene along with convenience. Not being able to enter a building because you have forgotten your mask has become an issue for many individuals because they would now have to go into a shop to purchase a mask before going about their daily lives. When providing vending machines that dispense these items, you can add significant convenience to individuals.

Coffee vending machines have also made a breakthrough in the industry; with more businesses opting to add these machines in offices, they are becoming very sought after. You can provide clients with tabletop vending machines or free-standing vending machines depending on their needs and the workforce who are using the machines.

Another big consideration is supplying your community with ATM vending machines. In these areas, the name suggests vending machines that dispense cash instead of snacks or sodas. Just like any other vending machine, you would need to restock your ATM vending machine, but instead of having to purchase items, you simply restock it with $20 bills. Every time an individual withdraws funds from your ATM vending machine, their financial institution will transfer the money into your account. You can apply the following tips should you consider investing in ATM vending machines:

- Place them in well-lit locations

- These vending machines need to be placed in areas with a lot of foot traffic

- Try to keep your ATM vending machine away from glass windows to increase security

- Have your ATM vending machine secured to the floor by a professional

- You would need a dedicated phone line and power outlet within three feet of the vending machine

- Ensure that you have cash ready when visiting your location so you can refill it when needed

- Whenever possible, don't refill your cash cassette in public view

ATM vending machines do very well in places like nightclubs, amusement parks, casinos, or apartment buildings. It adds convenience to their lives because they can get cash on route to where they are going. You can talk to business owners about having these vending machines placed in offices for employees to use. Be sure that you get insurance before placing your vending machines and that your insurance policy covers the highest amount within your vending machine. You might be thinking about how you can make an income from these machines, but the simple answer is you can charge anywhere between $1 and $4 per transaction. Should your ATM vending machine be placed in the perfect location, the income you can generate will be quite significant. For example, should you charge $2 per transaction and your machine receives 20 transactions per day, then you can generate $40 in profit. This is pure profit as you may not have any other overheads that you would need to cover when operating these machines.

Another popular vending concept that is popping up more and more is the vending of bicycling equipment. With fitness becoming a bigger part of people's lives, they are always in need of the necessary equipment. Not to mention the fact that in certain countries cycling is one of the main modes of transport. Especially in these countries, the need for cycling vending machines can be quite lucrative when placed in the right locations. These vending machines often dispense the following products: gels, nutritional bars, CO_2 cartridges, tubes, cycling caps, gloves, lights, chain lube, multi-tools, tires, chamois butter, puncture kits, drinks, sunglasses, hand warmers, locks, rim tape, pedals, action wipes, local trail maps, and spoke repair kits.

The vending industry is growing more and more in the past few decades, and most vending ventures require a large to mid-range investment concerning equipment, products, and marketing. You can start looking at other ways of getting into the industry without having to invest a large sum of money. This is where honor box vending comes in. So you might be asking what Honor Box Vending is. Honor box vending is when you place cardboard or plastic containers with snacks or candy at a location and allow customers to purchase them using an honor system. Buyers can follow the instructions you place on the box to purchase these items, for example, three for $1, or 50 cents each. The main thing to keep in mind is that the customer will have free access to the products you provide, and you would need to trust them to make this system work. This is a great model should you want to get into charity work, because you can place a charity sticker on the box and let the customer know that you are raising funds for them and you would appreciate their support. This can significantly boost your existing vending machine business especially when you mention that it is your company hosting the collections. A good example of charities you may want to sponsor is the National Children's Cancer Society Charity Vending Program. Once again, I have to emphasize the point that you would need to trust the location and the customers to make this work so I would suggest talking to an existing customer and asking them to have someone look over your honor box while you are unavailable.

One of the most important things you can do for your vending machine business is to ensure that your vending route or locations are safe from other vending machine business owners. There are a few ways you can prevent competitors from entering your locations and taking away valuable business. I will be sharing the holy trinity of a successful vending business with you below. Although you might think that having a great machine will automatically give you great business, in reality, your vending machines are just the start of your business. The perfect vending machine will not give you anything if you don't have the perfect location to place it. The first way of ensuring that you will be servicing a vending location for a time is by offering excellent customer service. The main difference between various vending machine business owners is the level of customer service they provide, and this will ultimately help you prevent competitors from stealing your profitable locations. Savvy business owners know that mutually beneficial businesses will last for a long time; this means that you would need to show your customers that their business is important to you. You can achieve this by being willing and responsive to your customer and accommodating their requests with very short notice. The vending machine business relies heavily on word-of-mouth advertising, and if you make a good impression, the possibility of getting referrals increases. You need to take the time to build relationships with your customers, get to know your customers, and allow them to get to know you, this will build trust. You can enhance your customer service by following these steps:

- Perform preventive maintenance regularly to eliminate the downtime of your machines, this will also increase the lifespan of your machine. This will also help you to save money and build a good reputation with your clients.

- Be as responsive as possible when it comes to service requests, no matter what type of communication your customer uses to log the requests, you should attend to them within 24 - 48 hours. You may also want to provide your top customers with a direct 24/7 contact number so they can get a hold of you at any time.

- When you set a deadline for delivery, ensure that you are ahead of time. Delivering on time is expected, but should you deliver before the time you will stand out from the competition and make customers trust you even more. You might also consider installing software that will help you manage inventory so you can restock your vending machines before they completely run out of stock.

The next thing you want to incorporate into your vending machine business to ensure its success is optimization. Every location where you place your vending machine will have different traffic patterns, customer demographics, and product requirements. Optimizing the vending experience is essential and requires hundreds or thousands of decisions that need to be made. The process of optimization includes the following to be done:

- Manage inventory, you should ensure that you know which products are selling better in which location so these locations are restocked regularly. One day can make a significant difference in the experience a customer will have with the quality of your service.

- Maximizing your vending route efficiency while still keeping your running costs low will improve your overall profits. This includes maintenance to prevent possible breakdowns of your machines.

- Keep your stock rotating so you aren't left with dead stock, determine which products aren't selling as well, and replace them with something else alternatively, keep the amount that you have on hand as low as possible to prevent them from expiring.

Ensure that you are optimizing your revenue as well. Although it might be easy to manage your business when you have one or two machines, it becomes more difficult when you have half a dozen of them, each one with its own set of data that you need to keep track of. This is the time that you would need to consider investing in vending machine management software (VMS) to help you with the management of your business. The main goals you should have for your business are lower costs and satisfied customers. Vending machine software will help you automate your decisions, and it will reduce the uncertainty related to the business. VMS will also help you to manage inventory, identify consumer trends, manage routes, and keep track of cash. You will have more free time with the use of vending machine software that you can apply to other areas of your business, like customer service.

Commissions are something we have mentioned throughout the book, but what are they exactly and how should you determine what you should pay to your location owners or managers. There are vending machine owners who offer their location owners a portion of their profits in the form of commission to acquire the location. This is also a way to ensure that no other vending business owners can enter the location. There are a few vending machine business owners who first want to ensure that they will be able to cover the commissions with their return on assets (ROA) before entering into a commitment. There are a few benefits to offering your locations commissions for using their space. When increasing the commission rates you can also increase the unit price of the items you are selling, this can often increase your profits by almost double. Maintaining your machines will also lead to higher revenues and profits and this will help to cover the costs associated with managing routes. Paying commission to help you get an increased market share as well as help you to obtain larger locations. One valuable tip is when you are offering a commission to a location try and stretch your contract to a minimum of 2 or more years.

You would need to determine what rate of commission you are willing or can afford to pay before you approach a client with a proposal. When entering a new location with existing vending machines you may want to try and offer a higher commission rate because you may not have a second chance to persuade the client. Obtaining a new client could mean that you would need to offer at least 20%, but you would need to ensure that the prices of your vending goods can cover this commission.

By now you might be wondering if there are other ways you can earn an income in the vending industry that doesn't involve you having to manage routes and restocking machines. One way you can make money is by flipping run-down machines. Should you possess the right set of mechanical or electrical skills you can purchase older machines that need a bit of love and attention and sell them for a profit. These machines may need a new coat of paint, some cleaning, and a firmware update that includes a note reader to be flipped for a profit. You may also want to look at the gas levels of the machine to figure out if you would need to re-gas the machine or if it is still fine.

Another way of earning additional income is purchasing existing routes, improving them, and selling them for a profit. You need to ensure that the machines on the routes are working properly and that you have adequate financial information related to the profits they can bring in, this is because potential buyers will want to see this information. You can sell routes you buy as clusters or as single units depending on the amount of profit you would like to make.

Chapter 8:
The Future Of The Vending Machine Industry

"Step out of the history that is holding you back. Step into the new story you are willing to create."

Oprah Winfrey

The future of technology

Ponder on different items to sell that may become (or have already become) more popular in the future (i.e., face masks/hand sanitizer) - of course, this would be pointless in Florida but would work better in NY, for example - because of people's preferences in different areas. Like real estate, this is all about location, location, location.

The future of the vending machine industry has grown and evolved quite a bit over the past few years. One question you would need to ask yourself is, if you are ready, should the vending industry go completely cashless. Would you be able to convert your existing machines to accept digital/card payments should a time come around where cash is no longer used? You need to consider this when purchasing your vending machines, especially when buying used machines or existing routes with standing vending machines. Converting vending machines is not as expensive and making the conversion could be much more profitable than working with cash vending machines. You may need to start doing your research now as to how to convert your machines should you still have coin/cash-operated machines.

With technology and currency changing so drastically, the possibility of cash being converted to digital currency is growing ever larger. The question is will you be ready should this happen and will you be able to adapt to this massive change in the economy? The main reason for the possible change in the world's currency is both technical susceptibilities and human error. The rise in bank hackers has become very worrisome to many individuals and for that reason, more individuals are making the change to digital currency. A central bank digital currency (CBDC) will also improve the current payment system while reducing costs and complexity. You might be wondering what a central bank is? Simply put a central bank is an institution that is given privileged control over the production and distribution of money and credit to individuals. This can then be used by individuals instead of using cash.

Customer behavior regarding the way they make payments has changed significantly over the past few years and you would need to adapt quickly to ensure that your business stays on top of the latest trends.

"Adding the cashless option makes a vending machine more popular because there are more ways to pay. Imagine a group of teenagers wanting to purchase soft drinks. If one of them needs cashless payment and the machine doesn't offer it, the entire group might walk past

and buy elsewhere. If you add cashless vending, that entire group can use the machine, including both cashless and cash users. Both types of sales, therefore, increase."

Paresh Patel

There are a variety of digital payments available at the moment and ensuring that your vending machines can accept some or perhaps all of them is imperative to the success of your business. I will be discussing each method in detail below:

Card Payments: Although more and more individuals are making use of card payments, this does not necessarily mean that the use of cash will be eliminated. Being able to pay for smaller items using your debit/credit card has indicated better infrastructure and openness.

"People hold more cards and use them more often. The average number of payment cards (e.g., credit and debit cards) per person in CPMI member countries rose from 1.1 to 2.5 in the 2007-16 period. Cards issued by EMEs drove this increase, as cards per person were little changed in most advanced economies. The frequency of card use increased from around 60 transactions per person on average in 2000 to close to 85 in 2016. In Australia, Korea, Sweden, and the United States, the average person uses a card more than 300 times per year, while in India and Mexico the number is less than 25 times a year."

Paresh Patel

There is no doubt that card payments are increasing, but saying with certainty which countries are bound to go cashless first is quite difficult to determine.

Although chip-and-pin options are used widely, contactless card payments will be the way of the future.

Mobile Payments

With the increase in technology, mobile payments have taken over card payments in a significant way. With over 87 million people using Apple Pay all around the world, retailers have to adapt to accept these forms of payment to receive payments. Mobile payments have increased by 47%, with smartphone owners who are using mobile wallets to make payments. WeChat pay currently has 600 million users, and Alipay is close behind with over 400 million users. Although this method of payment is still developing, it's only a matter of time before it will become the only means of payment.

"One reason for the slow rate of adoption in vending is that operators have already equipped thousands of machines with card readers, and they do not necessarily see the benefits of introducing mobile payments. For new locations, however, it can make sense to accept mobile payments, along with card payment capability."

Nick Montano

When switching your vending machine to accept all major cashless payment methods, you can make use of the Nayax Vpos Touch. It can be fitted to nearly all existing vending machines quickly and easily to ensure that you will not be losing out on any potential sales due to the lack of payment methods accepted by your machines. This device is a contactless card reader that accepts payments from credit/debit cards as well as pre-paid cards, mobile apps, QR codes, contactless, and swipe transactions. It also helps to secure communications and aids in monitoring inventory and cash as transactions are made. The device has a color touchscreen that is fitted with Gorilla glass that keeps it safe, and it has voice capabilities to ensure everyone can access it. Installing these mechanisms does not mean you would need to eliminate the acceptance of cash, and can be used along with cash transactions. This is purely one of the options available to convert your machines to accept various methods of payment, but you can do more research regarding the options available.

Tax

Another thing that has affected the vending industry is the introduction of a sugar tax. If you haven't heard, a sugar tax is new legislation introduced to reduce childhood obesity and use money received to fund sports and clubs. Manufacturers have, however started reducing the amount of sugar they add to their products to avoid paying these taxes. This does however aid in the goal that this tax is aiming to achieve. The sugar tax covers all types of sugar from sucrose and glucose to fructose and lactose. Keep in mind that it doesn't apply to drinks that are:

- At least 75% milk
- Milk replacements
- Alcohol-free drinks
- Sugar-free fruit and vegetable juice
- Drink flavoring added to drinks like coffee
- Powder drinks
- Mixed liquids like cocktails

- Infant formula or baby foods

- Diet replacements, dietary foods used for medical purposes

One way to reduce or avoid paying sugar tax on products is by supplementing the products you are currently supplying your customers with a healthier and lower sugar option. This not only allows your clients to eliminate unhealthy foods from their diet but can also help your bottom line and keep your profits up. You may not feel the pinch of the sugar tax immediately but it may have an impact on your business over the long term.

Inflation Risks

With inflation rates spiking due to problems we are facing in the world, you need to consider this within your vending machine business. Inflation can affect everything from gas prices to food prices, and the way that clients are using your services. Making provisions for changes with inflation is important when managing your vending machine business. For example, let's say inflation is 7% per year, you would need to increase the prices of your products during the price increases to ensure profitability is stable. Increasing prices after inflation could be detrimental to your profit margins and could lead to you losing quite a significant amount of money. Should you still have products in your machines based on prices before inflation, I would suggest waiting until your machines are almost sold out before restocking and increasing your prices to ensure customer satisfaction is kept intact. One thing to keep in mind in the vending machine industry is that the products you sell from your vending machines have to pay for your gas, maintenance, and purchase of new stock. Due to this, you would need to ensure that your profits can cover all your expenses. You may also want to put a notification on your vending machines informing customers that there will be an annual increase in prices at a certain time to not lose your returning client base.

You might be wondering how much you should increase the prices of your products, although this would depend on where you purchase your stock from, I would suggest keeping the inflation in mind. You might need to re-evaluate how much your supplier is planning to charge you for your most purchased products and if they can provide you with an updated price list. According to what your supplier would now be selling the products for you can start to restructure your prices to factor in the inflation increase. Inflation can range from year to year, and knowing what the planned increase is, is important because then you can plan according to that. You might not need to increase your prices by 7% as per the approximate yearly increase should you receive a discounted price from your supplier. You would need to consider what your competitors are charging and keep your prices in line with them so your location may not be taken over by someone else.

Another obstacle to keep in mind is if there is another lockdown and individuals will not be able to access your vending machines to purchase their favorite snacks. Should this happen again, and you are worried about suffering from potential profit loss? Then you might want to consider targeting locations within apartment complexes or companies considered to be essential services. This might be a bit more difficult as these locations often already have vending machines but not impossible if you can provide a better service and better quality to the location owner. You would need to keep this possibility in mind when opening your vending machine business as it might be a short-term solution to a long-term problem. The situations we are facing now are not going to change anytime soon, so planning for the worst from the start could mean the make or break of your business.

I have discussed risks that you might encounter in previous chapters of the book like theft and vandalism but let's look at some of the other risks associated with starting this business.

Monetary Risks: Although getting into the vending business requires little capital investment, the amount that you invest is still money lost should you not manage your business appropriately. Before spending money on vending machines, you would need to ensure that you are not being careless with your operations. Careless reasons can include investing in defective machines, traffic-prone locations, unpopular products, or turnkey vending businesses that may be running at a loss.

Commitment Risks: Although the vending business requires very little commitment, you still need to make time to spend on your business to ensure that it is profitable. You need to ensure the time you spend at your vending machines is quality, especially when refilling products, doing maintenance, and cleaning machines. If you don't make this a priority your machines may be running at a loss and you could lose your business because of neglect. You should always be prudent and proactive in your business to ensure it is moving in the right direction.

Legal Risks: Refer to previous chapters about all the legal documents you will need in your vending machine business.

Security Risks: Refer to previous chapters about how to secure your vending machines against vandalism and theft.

Chapter 9:
Re-Investing & Scaling Your Business to Six-Figures a Year

"I talk a lot about taking risks, and then I follow that up very quickly by saying, 'take prudent risks.'"

Irene Rosenfeld

As your business evolves, you might be asking yourself if you should be hiring employees to help manage your business? Where you can get individuals to help you out, how to teach them, how to make sure they don't steal, etc. You may also be wondering how many employees you may need to handle all your machines? Should you have one employee to manage, for example, ten of your machines or one per 20 machines? How many of your locations will they be able to cover? These are all questions you would need to answer before increasing the number of vending machines you own and acquiring more locations. Trying to operate a business consisting of 100 vending machines may become a bit more difficult if you are the only employee.

I think everyone can agree that finding people who you can trust to help run your business can be challenging, especially when there is money involved. For this reason, consider talking to close friends and family first and see if they will be willing to help you run your business.

Everyone is looking for extra income and you can be sure to find someone willing to help you out in their spare time to collect money, restock products, and maintain machines. As your business expands, you can start outsourcing individuals to assist in the daily running of your business. Another way of ensuring that you are employing trustworthy individuals is by employing an assistant to work with you out and build a relationship with them so you can determine if they can work on their own. This way of employing someone is helpful with the training aspect of running a vending machine business as well. Because the person working with you will be able to see what you do regularly they can learn by doing. This cuts down on training time and will have your employee ready for when you decide to sit back and have them do the work for you. a business consisting of 100 vending machines may become a bit more difficult if you are the only employee.

This cuts down on training time and will have your employee ready for when you decide to sit back and have them do the work for you.

When it comes to the number of employees you may need to assist you with your business, it would depend on the locations of your vending machines and how many you have that need regular check-ins. You would need to think about traveling when making this decision. For example, should you have 10 vending machines within a 20 km radius, then you might want to consider hiring only one person to man them all because not all of the machines would need to be serviced daily. But when we are looking at 20 machines spread out over a 100 km radius, then you might want to consider employing two individuals to help man these machines and make sure they are not too far from the locations. The reason why I am suggesting one person for every 10 vending machines is because they will be able to service 2 machines a day, rotating them every week depending on needs. Assigning more machines to one person may lead to machines not being adequately maintained, leading to profit loss.

Another big question many vending machine business owners have is how often they should assess the profitability of their vending machines. You can do this by setting up an excel spreadsheet and updating it as soon as possible. As with any business model, you would need to keep track of your income and expenses regularly to ensure you are moving forward and not backward. This means checking your spreadsheets at least three to four times a week until you have determined that you are making a profit. There are a variety of samples of excel spreadsheets you can use and adjust according to your specific needs and requirements.

The moment your vending machine business is starting to bring in a significant amount of profits per month, you might be asking yourself what you should do with your profits. There are various investments you can make with your vending machine profits, including stocks, cryptocurrencies, or investing in new machines and locations. Deciding what you would want to do with the profits you are receiving from your vending machines is a personal choice to make, but I would suggest investing in your business first. If you started your business with old used machines, consider purchasing newer models and switching them up, this could increase your profits and will show that your business is growing. You may also want to consider purchasing more machines or locations, which will also help to increase your profit margins. When you are happy with the number of machines and locations you have in your business, you can start looking into other investment opportunities. You can choose to invest in another vending machine business through stock investing. The vending industry is growing at a rapid pace, so even when you are not investing money into your own business, you can help other businesses and make an additional profit while running your own business. It's expected that the vending industry will grow by 6.7% per year between now and 2027, which means that you can get a significant return on your investment. These are, however, not the only types of stocks you can invest in (also consider commodities, ETF's, tech, etc.), and you can choose from a variety of businesses to invest in. Another potential way of accumulating more from your vending income is to invest some of that income in cryptocurrency. Researching both could help you to decide whether you should invest in them for the long term.

While on the subject of what to do with the profits you receive from your vending machine business. It would be good practice to keep money aside when you need to replace your existing machines. You should also remember to set profits to the side for tax. So, when should you consider replacing your machines with new ones? Your older vending machines may be working great and bringing insufficient profits, but you would need to consider if upgrading them would be a better option. While I discussed how you can move your older vending machines into the digital age in previous chapters, some machines are not able to be as easily converted. You may also want to consider purchasing new machines when the cost of maintenance on your older machines is worth more than purchasing another machine. This doesn't necessarily mean you have to purchase a new machine; you can still purchase a new-used machine, meaning you would purchase a newer model vending machine that is being sold as used.

In this next section, I will discuss some of the biggest and most profitable locations for placing your vending machines. Although there is no proven way of finding the perfect location, you need locations where there is high foot traffic. Finding the best locations depends on a variety of factors and these will also determine the success of your business. Here are a few instructions on how you can spot the best locations. Taking a deeper look into customer behavior at specific locations is your first step to finding the perfect locations for your vending machines.

Impulsive Buying

One of the most unnoticed trends is possibly impulse buying. You can leverage the effects of impulse buying to your benefit should you place your vending machines in the right location, and offer the right products. Products need to be intriguing to clients in all aspects but specifically sight. Possibly the best example I can use is children, being attracted to colorful and bright items like toys. Ensuring that both your products and your vending machines are pleasant to look at could boost your sales significantly. Should you only be interested in targeting the younger generation then, you might want to place your vending machines in places like shopping malls, stationery shops, ice cream parlors, in parks, etc.

Utility

Placing your vending machines in locations where they are needed is essential to success. This may involve some trial and error, but it would be worth it in the end. An example of this is placing a vending machine in an office building because individuals are prone to looking for quick snacks as opposed to going out to find food. It makes it more convenient for them to purchase items in the building.

Waiting Areas

Waiting areas could include places like bus stops, airports, and railway stations. These locations often have more foot traffic, and people often want something to pass the time, so a vending machine could just be the solution to their problems. Supplying snack items is a great idea, this is because many individuals tend to eat when they get bored of waiting.

Now let's move on to finding these locations for your vending machine and how to know whether they will be profitable. When first installing your vending machine you may experience a novelty effect, which means you will see a peak in the performance of your vending machine for the first couple of months. You should expect this to calm down after a while as individuals will get used to the machine being there and not be as tempted to buy products from it anymore. You should, however, keep in mind that if your machine doesn't do well within the first couple of months then the chances of that location not being profitable is very good.

Ideally, large grocery stores, hospital waiting rooms, or high schools would be great locations for your vending business, but realistically they are possibly already taken by other companies. It is possible to get these locations for your vending machines, although it might not be very easy. You would need to have a lot of patience, time, money, resources, and nagging to gain these locations. To get into larger businesses like schools, call-centers, office buildings, or manufacturing plants you would need to offer better service, selection, prices, and commissions to meet the business owners' expectations. By offering these things, you might be able to persuade owners to switch to your services. These are the perfect locations for your larger and bulkier machines. With regards to your smaller machines like bulk candy machines, I would suggest speaking to car lots, car repair shops, salons, hardware stores, thrift stores, dollar stores, restaurants, and bars.

When you have established the best vending locations, you would need to set up a vending machine marketing proposal. This will show your clients what they can gain from using your services as well as what your responsibilities will be concerning your vending machines. You might be wondering how you can write a marketing proposal to pursue potential clients to switch to you. A comprehensive marketing proposal will consist of the following:

• **Mission Statement:** A mission statement needs to clearly state what your vending machine business is about and what products you will be selling. You also need to be clear about your target audience and include where you currently have vending machines placed.

- **Niche Market:** Next you would need to explain your niche and which machines you are focused on. You should also include which locations you are targeting and why you are targeting them.

- **Services:** You need to clearly state what services you will be offering to the business so customers can be aware of what to expect. You may also want to include how many different products you can supply and how clients will be able to purchase products (cash or digital payments). Also, include your business' plans for the future and how you are planning on improving your business and its operation to add more value to customers.

- **Marketing and Promotion:** Clearly state how you promote your business and how you are approaching the market. Include what marketing strategies you are currently using, like a business card or brochures to create awareness of your company.

- **Identifying and Understanding Competition:** Explain to the customer about the competition currently in the market and how you are above them with your product and service offerings.

- **Marketing Goals:** In short, explain what your marketing goals are for your business over both the short and long-term.

- **Result Monitoring:** How will you be monitoring your progress and how your business is doing as well as how you will work at improving your business.

This is a very basic outline, but it should include all the necessary information your clients need to make an informed decision about using your business as their vending operator.

Since the vending industry is gaining more popularity and more people are looking to enter the industry, the possibility of selling your vending machines/routes is growing ever bigger. Individuals looking for a vending route include people who just got fired from their job, someone looking for a part-time job, someone needing extra income, or an individual looking to start a family-owned business. You can use the following checklist when you are looking to sell your vending machine business; it doesn't matter what kind of vending machines you are looking to sell; the checklist will be the same.

The first thing you would need to do is ensure that your business complies. Your vending machines should be in working condition so the new owner can start operating immediately after purchasing the business. Should some of your machines need repair, you need to inform the buyer so they are aware of any maintenance they may need to do. You should gather the following information and place it in a spreadsheet or PowerPoint presentation for interested individuals to easily have access to it:

- How long has your business been operating?
- Company name, Office location, Web address?

- **Locations of each machine:** You need to list each location address, as well as what kind of machine is located at each location. You should also include how much income you are generating from each machine. Include the serial numbers, brand type, and mechanical specifics of each of the machines.

- **Gross income generated monthly in total:** This means the total amount gathered from all your machines before subtracting expenses. The net amount is the profits you make after subtracting expenses. You can now calculate all your gross income and net income for the entire business you are selling.

- **Sale price:** The sales amount for your vending machine is typically 70-100% of the gross annual income you are generating from your business. Keep in mind that your business will be worth more if your vending machines were purchased new and not older than two years.

- **Extras:** You can now add in any extras, for example, established routes that you have had for more than five years. You should also include the market value of the extras you will be including in the sale of your business. These extras include your vehicles, cars, or vans. The equipment also includes hand dollies, coin mechanisms, changers parts, vendible products, and office supplies.

- **Training the buyer:** You can offer to train the buyer of your business. The price you will be charging for this depends on the experience the buyer has and how large your vending machine route is. Training can last anywhere from two days to two weeks. Some buyers would want to have a look at the vending machines and locations before purchasing your business, they may also want to talk to managers to introduce themselves.

• **Business bill of the sale-purchase agreement:** You can get a Bill of Sale Purchase agreement online or at your local "officemax" or office supply store in the business section. You and the buyer of your business would need to sign the document, and you can opt to have a notary public stamp to make the document legit; this is the sale process as when you are buying and selling a car.

• **Upfront payment:** You can accept two types of payments for your business; Money order or Cashiers check. When accepting a check, you might want to wait for the check to clear before handing over the keys to your business.

• **Financing:** When the individual looking to buy your business needs financing, they can contact one of the following institutions:

○ ACC Vendor Services

■ A dedicated partner offering leasing solutions for purchases under $350,000.

■ Offer designated professionals who will work with you and the buyer.

■ Their processes work through customized automation

■ They offer comprehensive lease training programs to help increase your sales opportunities.

o ACG Equipment Finance: An innovative leader in financing and leasing of business equipment. They provide quick and efficient loans for any type of equipment, and they are committed to customer satisfaction.

o Firestone Financial: An independent, direct lender providing financing for equipment and vendor financing solutions. Aids both indoor and outdoor amusement, vending, commercial laundry, and fitness industries.

o Paramount Financial: Offers competitive equipment financing in the United States.

o Superior Commercial Funding: Offers 100% unsecured financials for any business type. They do not need any upfront fees, and funding is released within 30 days of approval.

The next question you might have is where you can sell your vending machine business or vending routes. There are various websites available where you can advertise your vending machine business and the routes you want to sell. Some of the ones I found are:

- Vendingconnection.com
- Bizquest.com
- Businessesforsale.com
- Buybusiness.com
- Usedvending.com

The next thing you need to consider is the selling price of your vending business/route. This is not simply based on the profit you are making every month but is based on a variety of factors, as mentioned earlier. You may want to get a business valuation done before you consider advertising your business to ensure you are receiving what your business is worth.

There are various other ways of generating an income that you can use to boost your vending machine or increase your personal earnings. I will give you a few examples here, which will lead to the next chapter about creating a faceless YouTube channel to create passive income. The first investment opportunity I would like to talk about is cryptocurrency.

Buy and hold cryptocurrencies are often the popular choice amongst investors because you hold onto the shares you have bought until they gain a fair market share. Some of these cryptocurrencies are:

- Bitcoin
- Ethereum
- Binance Coin
- Chainlink

These cryptos can be held for the long term because they *COULD* (but are in no way guaranteed to) appreciate faster than the USD, EUR, etc.

Without going into detail on staking, De-Fi, and othe cryptocurrency endeavours, just understand and do some research on this area. At the time of writing, the market is crashing, and bitcoin has gone from a high of $67,000 all the way down to $20,000. Bear markets may give a better point of entry than buying during phases of hysteria.

Another popular part-time venture individuals are entering into over the past few years is creating branded clothing. This can even be incorporated into your vending machine business because you can create t-shirts and offer them to your clients or location owners/managers. Alternatively, you can create a print-on-demand store and create your clothing brand to sell to individuals. Printify is possibly the best website for creating a print-on-demand store because all you would need to do is set up your storefront and when clients order your merchandise the company will print their apparel and deliver it to the client. Alternatively, with the vending industry already booming and various vending machines making their appearance you can create a clothing brand and dedicate one of your vending machines as a clothing dispensing vending machine. This can be very lucrative and may earn you a great deal of extra income.

Should vending become your passion, you can opt to start a podcast where you can inform your followers about the newest trends related to the vending industry. Podcasts are becoming more popular as individuals are looking for informative content that they can listen to. Very few individuals have time to read and they prefer to listen to their favorite authors on platforms like Audible and Spotify and still get value for their money. Podcasts are also a great way of creating exposure for your company, informing business owners about the products and services you have to offer.

Another unrelated way of supplementing your vending machine income is through real estate investing, there are a few different ways in which you can achieve this which I will discuss in more detail below:

The first and possibly the most easy way of investing in real estate is through a real estate investment trust (REITs), and it's for a very good reason. A REIT can easily be bought through your regular brokerage account, IRA, 401(k), or another retirement account. These are traded publicly and regulated by the Securities and Exchange Commission. These trusts offer you high liquidity which allows you to buy and sell them instantly and diversifying them is easy because you can spread your investment among hundreds or thousands of properties or projects throughout the world. REITs must payout at least 90% of their profits in the form of dividends.

Another great way of getting into real estate investing is through owning or managing rental properties. Although these have their own set of advantages and disadvantages, they are still a great way of generating great revenue. With rental properties, you can predict the cash flow that the property will provide including the return on investment. When owning a rental property, you will be able to predict your expenses in advance like your annual repair costs, vacancy costs, vacancy rates, property taxes, property management fees, and insurance. You will have complete control over the property you choose, the tenants, and the management practices you use. You will also benefit from tax benefits when owning real estate, for example, writing off your mortgage interest, property management costs, and insurance.

Some of the disadvantages of owning rental properties are, for example, that they are very illiquid, meaning that you cannot sell them as quickly as you can buy them. They may also cost a lot to buy, even when you decide to take a mortgage for your property. Another major disadvantage of owning rental property is the management of the property itself, unless you hire a property manager, you could expect a 3 am wake-up call from tenants who are experiencing problems with the drains, for example.

Apart from rental properties, you can also opt to purchase a vacation property, which is ultimately a short-term rental property. These rentals require a lot more work due to the cleaning of the units before and after guests arrive or leave, marketing, coordinating entry, and communication with guests. You can, however, earn a larger amount of profits through short-term rentals and you will have access to a vacation home that you can use as you please, but you would need to have the right mindset for it. You need to make sure you triple-check all the numbers before you invest in a short-term rental property to ensure that you will not be running at a loss once you launch your vacation rental.

The above examples are some of the best extra income opportunities that you may consider doing to help boost your income alongside your vending machine business. These can all be highly profitable if managed correctly.

Chapter 10:
A Potential New Business Model For 2022/2023

The following chapter is a sample from our upcoming book: Youtube Millionaires – it's unrelated to Vending Machines, so if you are not interested in hearing about this opportunity, please stop reading here & instead, skip forwards to the Conclusion. Thank you.

In this chapter, I will be discussing how you can make an extra income through YouTube. YouTube has become the go-to platform for generating extra income and more individuals are looking to enter the industry. You can incorporate your vending business with a YouTube channel to increase your profits or you can create a YouTube channel as an additional income stream.

Faceless YouTube channels have grown more popular, and individuals are reaping the rewards of creating content without having to show their faces. Another benefit of faceless YouTube is that your videos can be reposted without them having to worry about copyright infringements, meaning that your channel will get even more exposure leading to higher revenue. All you would need to do to ensure your channel grows and gets viewed is ensure that the information you are providing to your viewers is valuable, this will ensure that you get repeat views. You might be wondering about having to still do voice overs on your videos, but it's very cost effective to hire narrators on Upwork.

So let's get into how you can start a YouTube channel.

You might be thinking about starting a YouTube channel but may be shy about showing your face on camera, but the realization is that you can start a faceless YouTube channel. I will discuss some of the niches you may want to consider when you are looking to create a faceless channel.

• **Life Hacks:** This first niche is very broad, and this means you can start with simple life hacks all the way to a bit more complicated content. People are often looking for ways to create more convenience in their lives and if you can provide it to them you are guaranteed to gain subscribers and advertising revenue your channel.

• **Health:** Health, just like life hacks have become a very popular niche for YouTube creators. The reason behind this is that individuals are often looking to self-diagnose themselves instead of heading to the doctor for just anything. These types of videos often only require equipment like a microphone for recording voice overs, stock clips or images, a video editing program, video transition, and title resets.

• **Food:** Another very popular niche especially when you can create simple and easy meals for people in a hurry. We all know life is already hectic enough without having to stand in front of a stove for hours preparing meals. Many people are often looking for easy and convenient meals to speed up their evening routines. Another route you might want to consider when starting a food YouTube channel is dedicating your content to junk food from around the world and teaching people how to make their own homemade takeaways.

- **Gaming:** Gaming has become a growing niche for YouTube creators, you can make use of other people's gaming clips (if allowed) and transform them into your content.

- **Psychology:** You can make psychology videos using stock photos and adding interesting titles to each. Psychology could help you gain quite a significant amount of subscribers as, once again, it is an often searched-for topic.

- **Luxury:** The luxury niche YouTube channels often focus on the most expensive watches, helicopters, sports cars, mansions, and superyachts. These channels show individuals what it would be like to live a rich life and what certain things in life cost.

- **Science:** When targeting children, especially early teens, you might want to consider creating a faceless science channel on YouTube.

- **Horror:** Creating videos of scary places you have visited or found on the internet can be extremely lucrative. Many individuals are looking for that blood-pumping experience and your content could be just what they are looking for.

- **Sport:** If you are a big sports fan, then this might be the niche for you. You can create content about international sports, different sports types, fitness, or wellness. You can commentate on filmed content or photos you found online and provide interesting facts regarding them.

• **Travel:** Did you know that you can create a travel channel without actually having to travel to different locations. Some individuals create content about amazing places in the world without leaving their homes.

• **Self Improvement:** Talking about self-improvement concepts can be extremely lucrative especially when the information you pass on to your viewers is life-changing. With these types of channels, you can once again use stock photos and create informative captions for your viewers.

• **Cryptocurrency:** A popular trend right now, and many individuals are currently looking for easy ways to enter and maintain their cryptocurrency investments. Once again you can use stock photos or you can position your camera towards your computer while doing tutorial videos. You can also do informative content about the most popular cryptocurrency investment trending.

• **Music:** You can create content related to the music industry and news about the latest artists and rappers. Individuals who are interested in music and what is going on in the industry will gladly subscribe to your channel should your content be informative.

• **Technology:** There are a variety of new gadgets on the market today and many individuals aren't aware of half of them. Creating YouTube content telling individuals about these technological advances could mean that you will gain quite a few subscribers.

- **Animals:** Informative content about the different kinds of animals around the world or the different breeds of dogs or cats can be very amusing for individuals to watch. This content is very popular at the moment and is well sought after.

- **Business:** Another great idea for content is talking about business. You can do anything from how to start a new business, how to increase sales, and so much more. You can create content on a variety of topics when you have business in mind and they are guaranteed to gain views.

- **Cars:** With new cars being released every few weeks there are no limitations on the amount of video content you can make on this niche.

- **Celebrities:** Another extremely interesting niche. Everyone is looking for the newest and hottest information about their favorite celebrities.

- **Mystery:** Similar to horror or scary content you can create thrilling mystery videos to entice your viewers.

- **Archeology:** A specialist niche that may have a targeted audience but can still be lucrative when you can reach them with your videos.

- **Aircraft and Airplanes:** Yet another specialized field of content but can still bring in lucrative income should you attract the right audience.

- **Ships and Boats:** This is an interesting topic since you can talk about anything from small boats to huge yachts and even include yachts owned by loved celebrities.

- **ASMR:** This has been a growing content niche and more people are looking for new ASMR content to watch. You can take content from TikTok and make a compilation or create your own unique content.

- **Quiz:** Quiz-related content can be anything from personality tests, giving individuals an idea of the type of personality they have. These videos often consist of animations and voiceovers.

- **House Walkthroughs**: This is a great idea should you be a realtor looking to show potential clients a house you have on the market.

- **Drawing:** Drawing content has been growing more popular over the past few years. Especially among the younger generation looking to learn how to draw simple pictures. These types of videos don't require any talking so you can opt to play some music while teaching your viewers how to draw.

- **Music Tutorials:** If you can play an instrument then filming tutorials or practice routines could be a great way of getting faceless content on YouTube.

- **Cooking Tutorials:** Similar to the food niche, you can film yourself preparing the food without showing your face on camera.

- **Software Tutorials:** One of the easiest faceless YouTube channels that you can start is one that showcases software tutorials. You are able to combine this niche content with affiliate marketing to increase your income.

You might feel a bit overwhelmed when you are considering the niche you would like your YouTube channel to be based around, but there are three main things you need to consider; what are you passionate about, what knowledge and skills do you have; is there an audience for my niche? Once you have answered these three fundamental questions, you can start working on finding a niche that will relate to these answers. Once you have listed out the various types of niches you can make content about there are three aspects to consider before choosing one; the audience, profitability, and your competition.

The audience you are targeting is the most important thing to consider before starting your channel. You can have a look at the market availability you have by checking the niche idea through search engine optimization. You can do this by searching for a keyword related to the niche you want to enter and seeing how many videos Google will show in your search feed. Keep in mind that just because a niche is popular, it doesn't necessarily mean that you will be able to profit from it. The next thing you would want to look for is the competition you may be facing when creating content and the type of content they are providing to their audience. You can compete by making your niche more specific to one genre. You can do this by not only talking about the general niche but being more specific, for example instead of talking about food in general, narrow your content down to food in a specific country or region. You should also be very careful about violating any laws that YouTube might set out.

Should you feel you are not good with words and you won't be able to say what you think on your YouTube channel, then you might want to consider getting content written for your channel. You can get in contact with freelancers who will write a script for you to read when doing voice overs. This is an effective way of making sure your content has valuable information and you are getting the intended message through to your viewers. You can search for freelance writers on sites like Fiverr who will happily assist you with writing a script based on your niche.

You might be asking how long you should make your video content, well the short answer is there is no prescribed length it depends on a variety of factors, including:

- The topics you will be covering
- The style of your video
- The subject of your video
- The audience you are targeting
- The devices your audiences are watching on
- And lastly yourself.

There are some statistics you can use as a guideline for the length of your videos, but I have to emphasize that the length depends completely on yourself and how you want your content to be interpreted by your audience. The average first-page YouTube video is around 15 minutes long, a channel based around beauty is around 10 minutes long, and the top ten YouTube channels have videos that are only three minutes long. Now based on these statistics and the advice of professionals your videos should be around 10-18 minutes long to grab your viewer's attention. Figuring out the ideal length of your videos will require that you know what your audience wants, try posting videos of around 15 minutes long and then asking your audience to let you know what length they would prefer. Do they want longer or shorter videos based on your content?

Before you consider starting a YouTube channel and making money from it, you should be aware of the guidelines that you need to follow. Keep in mind that YouTube is administered by Google, Alphabet Inc. YouTube reviews content through human reviewers and machine learning to ensure that content is within guidelines. These guidelines are in place to ensure YouTube is a safe community for everyone that watches the content that is uploaded. There are a few categories of community guidelines that you should be aware of:

- Spam and Deceptive practices
  - Fake engagement
  - Impersonation
  - External links
  - Spam, deceptive practices, and scams
  - Playlists
  - Additional policies
- Sensitive Content
  - Child safety

- Thumbnails
- Nudity or sexual content
- Suicide or self-harm
- Vulgar language
- **Violent and Dangerous Content**
- Harassment or cyberbullying
- Harmful or dangerous content
- Hate speech
- Violent criminal organizations
- violent or graphic content
- **Regulated Goods**
- Firearms
- Sale of illegal or regulated goods and services
- **Misinformation**
- Misinformation
- Elections misinformation
- Covid-19 medical misinformation
- Vaccine misinformation

In addition to the general guidelines that you need to follow you should also be wary of the monetization policies. These policies have been set in place to limit the number of spammers, impersonators, and bad actors. To monetize your YouTube channel, you need to be part of the YouTube Partner Program (YPP), to apply for membership you need to meet the eligibility requirements related to watch time and subscribers. When YouTube reviews your content after you apply for admission into YPP, they will check for the following:

- Main theme
- Most viewed videos
- Newest videos
- Watch time
- Video metadata (titles, thumbnails, and descriptions)

Should you not meet the requirements listed above or you violate any of the policies, then YouTube may take action the following actions to stop the monetization of your channel:

- **Turn off ads to your content:** When you become a member of YPP you can turn on ads to your content, yet when you don't meet the guidelines YouTube has set out they can turn off ads from your content.

- **Suspend participation:** YouTube can suspend you from taking part in the YouTube Partner Program completely and can also disable all of your accounts.

- **Suspension or Termination:** To protect the platform and the viewers, YouTube can decide to terminate your channel.

- **Inform:** YouTube will inform you in writing via email should they take any of the above steps towards your channel.

Another thing you need to be aware of is the countries covered under the monetization partner program before starting your channel. When you are using YouTube to promote your products and services (given they are within the guidelines) then you can do it from anywhere. The following countries are covered under the monetization partner program:

Algeria

Argentina

Australia

Austria

Azerbaijan

Bahrain

Belarus

Belgium

Bolivia

Bosnia

Herzegovina

Brazil

Bulgaria

Canada

Chile

Colombia

Costa Rica

Croatia

Cyprus

Czech Republic

Denmark

Dominican Republic

Ecuador

Egypt

El Salvador

Estonia

Finland

France

Georgia

Germany

Ghana

Greece

Guatemala

Honduras

Hong Kong

Hungary

Iceland

India

Indonesia

Iraq

Ireland

Israel

Italy

Japan

Jamaica

Jordan

Kazakhstan

Kenya

Kuwait

Latvia

Lebanon

Libya

Liechtenstein

Lithuania

Luxembourg

Macedonia

Malaysia

Malta

Mexico

Montenegro

Morocco

Nepal

Netherlands

New Zealand

Nicaragua

Nigeria

Norway

Oman

Pakistan

Panama

Paraguay

Peru

Philippines

Poland

Portugal

Puerto Rico

Qatar

Romania

Russia

Saudi Arabia

Senegal

Serbia

Singapore

Slovakia

South Africa

South Korea

Spain

Sri Lanka

Sweden

Switzerland

Taiwan

Tanzania

Thailand

Tunisia

Turkey

Uganda

Ukraine

United Arab Emirates

The United Kingdom

United States of America

Uruguay

Vietnam

Yemen

Zimbabwe

As I have mentioned before, you can create Youtube content by using stock images, but you can use stock videos as well. Several websites give you access to copyright-free stock videos that you can download and use for your content. I have found 12 of the best websites you can use:

- **Pixabay:** They offer over 2.3 million videos and images that are free to download and use. Some of the images may have a list of what is not allowed with images, but most are free to use. The videos you can download range from 12 seconds to one-minute lengths.

- **Videvo:** Another great site to use for free stock video footage, although they also offer graphics, music, and sound effects. Keep in mind that some of the content available may be licensed in a few different ways. They have three different license types including, Videvo Attribution License, which lets you use a clip for free, but you would need to pay the author, Clips with a creative common 3.0 can be used for free should you have credit, and Public Domain licenses that lets you use the content as you wish.

- **Pexels:** Pexels offer a wide range of free stock videos that you can edit and modify as you please. They also give you the option to look at trending free stock videos, so you can be up to date with what is currently trending.

- **Videezy:** This site also offers a variety of royalty-free video clips for personal and commercial use, although some of the videos would require that you credit videezy.com when using their content. You can however purchase credits that allow you to use the videos without attribution.

- **Life of Vids:** Collection of free stock videos, clips, and loops. This site has no copyright restrictions but you are limited to 10 videos when you are planning to redistribute the videos on other sites.

- **Coverr:** This site has thousands of free videos that have been downloaded over five million times. The videos are free to use for personal and commercial purposes.

- **Splitshire:** Created by Daniel Nanescu, this site offers photos and videos that are free to use for personal and commercial use.

- **Clipstill:** Clipstill is one of the sites that have a membership plan for unlimited download that costs $49. Although they have content that is free to download and use.

- **Dareful:** Dareful has a few hundred stock videos to choose from that are royalty-free. Their content is however licensed under creative commons 4.0 which means that you would need to give credit to the site and mention if you made any changes.

- **Vidsplay:** With new videos being added every few weeks, this site has a comprehensive collection of royalty-free videos for you to choose from. You do however need to give attribution when using this site's content.

So we have covered the topic of video content, scriptwriters, and how you monetize your videos. Let's discuss the topic of employing a voice-over artist to narrate your videos and give it that extra something special. Choosing the right voice-over artist may however be a little more difficult because every person has a different way of interpreting voices and you would need to find someone who will speak directly to your audience and make an impact on them. You can follow the tips below to make sure you find the right voice over artist for your videos:

Keep your target audience in mind: Consider the age of your audience, you can determine this through testing and market research. You would need to appoint a voice-over artist who will appeal to your target audience.

Accent: The accent of your voice-over artist is important to consider, especially when you are targeting an audience from another country.

Gender: This one is quite obvious, you might not want to consider a female voice-over artist should your target audience be mainly male individuals. Where neutral videos are involved it wouldn't matter if you choose a male or female artist. Female voices are often more popular because of their nurturing, compassionate, helping, and non-threatening tone.

Voice Tone: When speaking especially with voiceovers it's not about what you say but rather how you say it. Your voice-over artist should be able to deliver your message clearly to influence your audience. You should let your artist know what tone of voice you require for your content depending on the message or action you intend for your users to commit to.

Speed and Pace: The time limit is determined by the script for your video, this will determine the amount of information that needs to be added. Your voice-over artists should be able to align the video with the speech and find a balance between the two. You should also take a look at your artist's reading speed and not overload your script with too much information.

After considering all of the above requirements you will be able to appoint a voice-over artist who will make your videos stand out and attract a larger audience to your channel.

The following thing you should consider is your uploading frequency. Establishing a set schedule may be quite difficult with life taking priority and things happening unexpectedly. An ideal schedule will consist of 1-2 uploads a week but this will depend highly on the niche of your channel. A lot of time and effort goes into creating content for YouTube, you need to film, edit, and then upload it to YouTube. You need to consider this when deciding on your uploading schedule because you would need to have the time set aside to accomplish these tasks. Scheduling your content uploads is important because if you don't set specific days or times for your uploads your audience will start to get confused and this could lead to you losing views and harming your channel's future.

We all live extremely busy lives and the necessity to plan out our schedules is important, for this reason, it may be a good idea to put out your channel schedule on your social media pages so your followers know when not to expect a video from you. You can also work ahead of time by creating content a few days or weeks in advance so that when upload times come you have content ready to go instead of rushing around to get everything done. This will also help you to stay accountable for your YouTube channel and motivate you to upload your videos. And the final tip I have is that you set achievable goals for yourself and your channel. If you are aiming to upload four videos a week then you might be letting yourself down when you are only able to upload two. Be realistic with your goals and expectations and keep an open mind when you start your channel.

Now the final and most important question will be answered. How much can I make from a YouTube channel? This will depend highly on your channel analytics and how your channel is doing based on views and subscribers. Some of the most popular Youtube channels can make up to $10,000 per month. It does, however depend on the niche you choose and how popular it will be amongst viewers. Should your channel receive an RPM (Rate Per Mile) of $28.80 - then if your videos are getting 56 million views per month it would mean you could be making $14,000 per month. The math behind these calculations is quite difficult to understand, but the amount of money you can make isn't. YouTube is an extremely profitable platform and one thing to keep in mind is that YouTube doesn't pay you but rather the advertisers who use your channel. So for that reason, if an advertiser sees your content as something that could bring in sales for them then they will be more than happy to use your channel and pay you for it. Some of the most successful faceless and niche-specific cash cow YouTube channels at the moment are:

- Bright Side: With over 43.3 million subscribers and 8.8 billion views they specialize in content created around the life hacks niche.

- Bestie: This channel has over 4 million subscribers and they primarily use stock photos to create content. Their content is specific to the health niche.

- Top5Gaming: A channel with over 5.1 million subscribers and specific to the gaming niche. They have made their mark talking about games like Fortnite specifically and one of their most popular videos has over 1.7 million views.

- Brainy Dose: When looking at the psychology niche then Brainy Dose is possibly the biggest channel, they have over 1.67 million subscribers and cover a variety of topics on their channel.

- Smart Banana: Science has become very popular among the younger generation and with over 1.72 million subscribers this channel has made its mark on YouTube. They use mainly voiceovers and stock photos to create content and this has worked brilliantly for them.

- Nuke's Top 5: Considered to be one of the most popular niches right now, Nuke's top 5 has over 3,37 million subscribers and talks about everything creepy to get your blood pumping.

There are various channels from various niches that you can find on YouTube, but these are the top ones that I found for your perusal.

Now that you have all the information regarding monetizing your YouTube channel nothing should be stopping you from starting. You can make a significant amount of money from this side hustle if you follow the steps in this chapter.

Conclusion

I wrote this book with the intent to help as many individuals looking to start a vending machine business as possible. Vending is a great way of earning extra income and ultimately moving it into a full-time job. I am hoping that you found the information contained in this book interesting and informative and that you have learned everything you needed to know.

I have given you solutions to the most common problems you might be experiencing in your vending machine business, for example lack of money, wanting to start a business, quitting your job, unsure where to start, and how much it will cost. I have also provided solutions so you can be free from financial stress, a boring job, and a condescending boss. I hope that by reading this book you are attracted to the simplicity, predictability, and reliability of cash flow that this business will provide you with. You can start this business in your hometown, no matter how big/small your city, and you are intrigued with the idea of meeting new people and building strong relationships with your local business owners.

Throughout this book, you have learned the fundamentals of starting a vending machine business. I hope that through using the information contained here, you can start building your empire and reach your goals of financial freedom. I have covered everything about why you should start this amazing and ultimately profitable venture, but should you still have questions about how to start, please feel free to reach out to me. Researching your area and getting ready to launch your new business is important, so be sure that you are taking a good look around you and making notes about what you see.

I hope that you have learned that registering your business as an LLC is not only the best option for your business but also when following the steps contained in this book it's easy to achieve.

The tips contained in this book related to negotiation can help you gain valuable locations and dedicate customers. Remember that customer service and the image you present to customers are important when trying to tie down lucrative locations.

The operational management of your company including the security and profit margin within your business is of utmost importance when you want to be successful. Some insider secrets are exactly what you need to help motivate you to get your dream off the ground. Learning how to re-invest your business profits is another way of increasing your income and growing your business even faster.

Subscribing to the following blogs and forums will give you some helpful tips and help you solve some common problems you might encounter along the way. You may also want to read some of the following recommended books below to help you on your road to success.

If there is one thing that I would like for you to take away from this book it would be that starting a vending machine business is not just for the super-rich or already successful business owners, but that anyone can do it given the right motivation and information. This book is jam-packed with useful information that you can apply to your business.

When looking through social media to find inspiration related to your vending machine business, consider following the individuals listed below on Twitter:

• Markus Graham: Marcus Gram | Vending Machine Expert (@brothergram) / Twitter

• Uselectit Vending: Uselectit Vending (@uselectit) / Twitter

• Vending Machine Pirate: Vending Machine Pirate (@TacoZoo303) / Twitter

• Jamoooooo: Jamoooooo (@VendingJames) / Twitter

• Big Mon: Big Mon (@_MoneyMakingMon) / Twitter

• Stush Boss: STUSH BOS (@Samyonce_) / Twitter

• Richard Spencer: Richard Spencer (@468richards) / Twitter

There are many blogs that you can follow to find information regarding the vending business as well as useful tips and tricks to improve your business. You may want to subscribe to the following blogs:

- Bevco Service Inc Blog: Bevco Service - Blog - South Jersey Vending Machine News | BEVCO Service Inc

- Camelback Vending Blog: Blog - Camelback Vending

- Global Vending Group Inc Blog: Vending Machines for Sale | Buy Vending Machines Used, New (globalvendinggroup.com)

- Healthy You Vending: HealthyYOU Vending - Start a Healthy Vending Machine Business

- Vendnet USA Blog: Vendnet USA Blog | Vending Machine Parts, Vending Machine Repairs, and more!

- Planet Vending: Vending News from Planet Vending, UK Vending News & Events (planet-vending.com)

- Intelligent Dispensing Solutions: IDS | Vending Machine Manufacturer (idsvending.com)

- Automatic Food Service Blog: Automatic Food Service Blog - Vending Machines in Montgomery and Auburn (afsvend.com)

- Vending Group Blog: Vending Group Blog

- Vending World: Refurbished Vending Machines, Soda and Snack | Vending World

- Natural Vending Blog: BLOG | Vend Natural

- Vendsoft Vending Blog: Vending Blog - VendSoft

- Atlantic Vending Blog: Blog – ATLANTIC VENDING – New Jersey Vending Company (atlanticvendingnj.com)

- Ownr: How to Start Your Vending Machine Business | Ownr

- Logaster: Vending Machine Business From A to Z | Logaster

- Fora Financial: 6 Tips for Starting a Successful Vending Machine Business - FF Blog (forafinancial.com)

I have compiled a list of the most popular finance books for you to read when you are considering starting your own business. This list includes books about sales, taxes, persuasion, and more:

- To Sell Is Human - Daniel H. Pink

- Influence: The Psychology of Persuasion - Robert B. Cialdini

- Pitch Anything: An Innovative Method for Presenting, Persuasion, and Winning the Deal - Chen Kloff

- Never Split the Difference - Chriss Voss

- Secrets to Closing the Deal - Zig Ziglar

- The Ultimate Sales Machine - Chet Holmes

- The Art of the Pitch - Peter Coughter

- 50 Scientifically Proven Ways to be Persuasive - Robert B. Cialdini

- How to Pay Zero Taxes - Jeff A Schrepper

- 1001 Deductions and Tax Breaks - Barbara Weltman
- Taxes Made Simple - Mike Piper
- Simple Numbers, Straight Talk, Big Profits - Greg Crabtree
- Small Time Operator - Bernard B Kamoroff
- Small Giants - Bo Burlingham
- Mind Your Business - Ilana Griffo
- Will It Fly - Pat Flynn
- Taxes - For Small Businesses Quickstart Guide - Clydebank Business
- Company of One - Paul Jarvis
- Guerilla Marketing - Jay Conrad Levinson
- Supermaker - Jaime Schmidt
- Side Hustle From Idea to Income in 27 Days - Chris Guillebeau
- The Pumpkin Plan - Mike Michalowicz
- Getting Everything You Can Out of All You've Got - Jay Abraham
- The Young Entrepreneur's Guide to Starting and Running a Business - Steve Mariotti
- Rich Dad Poor Dad - Robert T Kiyosaki
- The Art Of The Deal - Donald Trump

The following are some of the best forums you can use to find information related to your vending machines and your business:

- Vending Chat: Vendingchat.com - All Vending Forums and Bulletin Board
- Vend Resourse: Forums | Vend-Resource
- Vendiscuss: VENDiscuss Forum

I would like to thank you for taking the time to read this book, and would love if you will leave a five-star rating on amazon if you found it valuable.